FEAR IS A THIEF

—⚋—

FIVE POWERFUL TRUTHS TO HELP OVERCOME YOUR BIGGEST FEARS

GARY WESTFAL

Westfal Publishing, LLC
Since 2012

A Subsidiary of
G-Life Enterprises Corp.

Copyright © 2017 G-Life Enterprises Corp.

All rights reserved. No part of this book may be reproduced, scanned, or distributed in any printed or electronic form without permission from the author and/or publisher, except by a reviewer, who may quote brief passages in a review or critique. Please do not participate in or encourage piracy of copyrighted materials in violation of the author's rights. Purchase only authorized editions.

To receive a free biweekly e-mail newsletter delivering relevant and personally empowering content about how to get more out of life, register directly at www.gwestfal.com.

ISBN: 978-0-9992220-2-7
LCCN: 2017914638

BOOK DESIGN BY: G-Life Enterprises Corp
Gary Westfal, Concept Art
Scott Grinnell, Graphic Artist

All image permissions have been secured and/or released for use by their originator or rightful owner and documentation is on file with the publisher.

Printed in the United States of America

Also by Gary Westfal

KEY HORIZON

DREAM OPERATIVE

This book is dedicated to those who find the courage to face their fears and dare to change their lives forever more.

Acknowledgments

Writing a book is an incredible undertaking. This is especially true when writing a book designed to empower people as opposed to entertaining them as I have done so far with two successful novels. I sincerely hope Fear Is a Thief inspires you, enlightens you, and empowers you to see past the fears that have been holding you back and keeping you from living the life you deserve to live on your terms.

My life has been a long and continuous process of personal and professional development that has brought forth the content found in this book. Presented in the form of fundamental truths, the information and ensuing wisdom have served me well and have helped me see past fear, casting clarity onto the horizon of my dreams, goals, and aspirations with new insight. These truths work for me and can work for you too.

The fundamental truths contained in the pages of this book are supported by story submissions from real people who have experienced their own fears or who were inspired by someone who helped them change the paradigm of fear.

While each story is unique unto itself, the commonality among them speaks to the reality of fear while offering an encouraging reminder that we are able to see beyond fear and step into the power we have over it.

I have spent a significant part of my life studying the masters of philosophy, enjoying thousands of hours listening to relevant content, practicing the concepts, and living a lifestyle principled by dominance over fear. The list of those who have influenced me is exhaustive. These great leaders, thinkers, and articulate writers and speakers have a gift. Their dedication to personal empowerment and the effect of their messages go far beyond that which even *they* will ever truly appreciate. Zig Ziglar, Mark Sanborn, Tony Robbins, Brian Tracy, Susan Jeffers, Andy Andrews, Jim Rohn, Jack Canfield, and Chris Widener are just a few of the names that have provided insight and inspiration toward writing this book. I live by a simple philosophy that wisdom, and the inspiration it instills, should be shared. From their wisdom to mine, I now pass it along to you.

To those who have inspired my passion to publish this book—friends both old and new, family, contributors, colleagues, and acquaintances—I thank you all. A special nod to my friend Larry Waddy, who was always "too blessed to be stressed." May God rest your soul. Your inspiration and your belief in me as a writer will be with me to the end of this life and the beginning of the next…where we shall meet again.

Table of Contents

Introduction *Fear Is a Thief!* xi

Chapter 1 *The Truth* 1

Chapter 2 *My Story By Gary Westfal* 7

Chapter 3 *The First Truth: Identify the Fear* 19

Chapter 4 *The Second Truth: Confront the Fear* 43

Chapter 5 *Blood, Sweat, and Fear*
           A Story by Scott Duke 61

Chapter 6 *Conquer the Darkness* 71

Chapter 7 *Butterflies, Birds, and Blossoms*
           A Story by Jan Waddy 91

Chapter 8 *The Third Truth: Replace the Fear* 99

Chapter 9 *The Fourth Truth: Redirect Your Focus* 115

Chapter 10 *The Fifth Truth: Be Patient…Be Strong!* 129

Chapter 11 *Armed and Prepared* 145

Speaking with Confidence
An Excerpt, by Larry Waddy 151

Our Contributors 155

About the Author 157

Introduction

Fear Is a Thief!

Fear. The very word has a menacing connotation with the power to conjure intimidating images that are mentally stored and categorized across the psychological spectrum. From spiders to speaking, ridicule to rejection, and ghosts to guns, our fears express our values and define the parameters of our lives, which can be every bit as liberating as they can be restrictive.

We live in a fear-based society not limited by geographic borders or global cultural differences. Fear indiscriminately affects everyone in some manner, shape, or form. Virtually every one of us has something we fear. This may be encouraging or discouraging, depending upon your perspective. But hold that thought, because it is the very essence of *perspective* from which fear gains its greatest power.

Life on the other side of fear is different. It is amazingly different! It is not governed or controlled by second-guessing, strategic pauses, or the false veil of perception we assign to our experiences. It is governed by truth, courage, and an ability to see things as they are instead of how we imagine them to be.

Let's call fear what it is, shall we? Fear is an enemy—a thief—that robs us of the things we rightfully desire for our lives. It hides behind the cowardly cloak of deception *we* permit *it* to wear, effectively allowing it to have more power than it rightfully deserves. The presence of fear can evoke physiological and psychological reactions ranging from a simple hesitation to outright paranoia. Some will argue that fear protects us from inherent danger. And there is a measure of truth to the statement, but only when it evokes awareness in lieu of an outright paralysis preventing us from experiencing the richness of life.

We fear so many things, giving so much credence to what we *perceive* is worthy of fear that we end up robbing ourselves of the full experience of life. We avoid steps inevitably leading to success and happiness because we fear the responsibilities that accompany success. Because we cannot reasonably predict an outcome or effect with certainty, doubt begins to set in. As doubt sets in, we become anxious. As we become anxious, fear begins to reveal itself. When fear is present, hesitation sets in. Each of these elements is a building block of fear's assault when it comes to preventing us from realizing success or happiness in any real and meaningful way.

One of our most prolific fears is the fear of the unknown. All we are afraid of, whatever it may be—loss, falling, drowning, flying, public speaking, judgment, embarrassment, rejection, dying, spiders, failure, and success—can be summarized into an all-encompassing common category of "the unknown." We are afraid of what we don't know, so we do our best to assume a likely outcome, which, in our minds at least, transforms it into something we *do* know and into something we *can* control. The result is typically a distorted perception of reality, the likes of which we go to great lengths to avoid.

We are afraid of what we *perceive* to be real because we are intuitively programmed for self-preservation and safety. We think in terms of worst-case scenarios until we discover it is "safe" to assume or operate otherwise. In doing so, most of us inaccurately posture ourselves to avoid such situations altogether. Our internal programming—designed to protect us from hurt and harm—can be the very element that prevents us from experiencing the fullness of life we would otherwise enjoy. The associated fear can keep us deceived and rob us of experiencing love, wisdom, healing, joy, prosperity, and the quality of life we rightfully deserve.

This book was written to address fear and to remind us all to take a moment to assess the validity of our initial judgment and perspective when it comes to our fears…or what we perceive to be fearful. Instead of rules, this book offers simple *truths* to live by that will help you look at fear in an entirely different way. The truths captured in the following pages will help you to better understand fear, enable you to live more courageously, and empower you to realize your full potential by allowing you to take control and see fear in its truest state. You will quickly realize that your fears are not always what they seem to be at first glance. This new perspective will become the basis of the courage you will discover in facing your fears by putting them in their rightful place. The principles—or *truths*—are supported by real stories from people who have faced their own fears in a variety of ways and in various circumstances. These stories were included to offer a sense of hope to those facing their own fears and to prove how fear can be effectively dealt with in a variety of ways, each empowering us to become stronger, wiser, and happier.

The fact is, we *all* have fears. Even the bravest among us has something he fears. To an outside observer, our fear may or may not have merit. Why is that? Because fear is a very personal experience built upon the *perceptions* we have created over a period of time. Those perceptions are formed in a variety of ways and can range from the manner in which we were raised to the experiences we have encountered along the path of our individual lives. And, until we *choose* to face the fear in order to mitigate, manage, or confront it, it will continue to be a part of our makeup, and we will continue to react on the basis of its dominance.

Notice that I used the word *choose* in the previous sentence. The mitigation, management, or confrontation of a particular fear must be a *choice* rather than a mere desire. Desire, by itself, is *not* enough to effect change. Change comes through choice. Choice induces action. And *action* produces change! It's an amazingly simple yet powerful axiom. There are many people who are quick to tell you what they *want* out of life but far too few willing to accept the changes that must accompany the desires they have. They fear change even though they proclaim change is what they desire. Fewer still actually proclaim what it is they are *doing* to achieve what they want. *Choose* to face your fear today, embrace change, and watch the world around you transform.

The fact that you have selected this book indicates you have acknowledged a need to take action to face your fears, or its premise offers a glimmer of intrigue for you to gain more insight on the concept of fear. In either case, you are to be congratulated on completing a very important first step. Take heart in knowing there is hope, no matter what your reasons for learning more about how to effectively deal with fear.

1
The Truth

Fear is transformative—it will always exist. I'm sorry if you find that discouraging or disappointing, but knowing this truth up front allows us to openly recognize and accept that each situation brings its own unique set of fears that must be effectively dealt with in order to move beyond hurdles or obstacles standing in the way of progress or personal growth. Without progress we become stagnant, bored, bitter, regressive, and…fearful. Don't allow fear to rob you of the victories. The fact that fear will always exist does not mean we cannot effectively deal with fear and overcome it.

This book will offer insight and methods to empower you with understanding, wisdom, and courage through a methodical approach of revealing basic truths designed to help you see fear for the thief it is.

For some of us, our fears were born from self-doubt, perpetuated by the overprotective nature of friends and family as they did their best to provide wise counsel along the path of our lives. Most of us listened and elected to adopt some of the very same fears as our advisers, legitimate or not. We chose to associate with some of the well-intentioned advice as much as we would like to think otherwise. And in so doing, we created a sense of doubt and self-pity that has manifested itself into the basis of what we perceive as fearful. As I mentioned earlier, some of these fears are so intimidating they conjure psychological and physiological side effects that can be quite debilitating. Just listen to the internal struggle between your desires and your "rational side" the next time you face a fearful situation, and you will be reminded of the varying levels of anxiety that exist.

The key to overcoming this internal struggle can be found in the pages of this book, which is designed to reeducate and reorient you to a proper position of power from which you will gain a totally new perspective on your fears. You will soon learn that, despite the good intentions of those who love and care for us, we do not have to live with the fears they helped us create. We will have plenty of opportunities to face our own fears as we make our way toward our dreams, goals, and desires. So, the less "acquired" fear we carry, the better off we will be.

If we are to effectively *manage* fear, we must make a conscious decision to take action to understand our fears. We must understand the methods and tactics that will lead to the overpowering of fear so we can regain control of our lives without making fear a dominant part of the equation. So, how do we do it?

I have discovered *five* fundamental truths for overcoming fear that are universal in nature. Apply these truths to put fear in perspective, and you will begin to effect real change in your life. These truths will help you discover how to overcome your biggest fears—fears preventing you from living the life you desire, fears preventing you from the full experiences of life. Each truth reveals practical insight into how to effectively deal with fear. Each one builds upon the others in ways that help you gain increasing confidence to face your own fears and develop your own unique approach to dealing with fear. These truths will provide an educational perspective you can apply to your own life *right now*. Some people have used these truths to:

- Improve and restore relationships
- Double and triple their incomes
- Lose weight, get in shape, increase overall physical well-being
- Reduce stress and overcome depression, despair, and helplessness
- Increase confidence levels leading to personal discovery, growth, and wisdom
- Discover the courage within that leads to rewarding changes and opportunities
- Provide an introspection leading to better focus, true happiness, and harmony

The truths you will discover in this book are supported by *real* stories from *real* people who have faced their fears. They have freely offered their stories in the hope that their words may somehow resonate with you to inspire, encourage, and empower you to take action. If you look closely, each story is supported in some way by some or all five of the fundamental truths. All of the stories are a testament to the *ultimate* truth that we can indeed live our lives free from the overwhelming grip fear sometimes has on us.

Yes, these five truths will reveal fear as the thief it is and lead you to a world of self-discovery and personal awareness, placing you in a position of dominance over the fears holding you back.

1. *Identify the Fear*
2. *Confront the Fear*
3. *Replace the Fear*
4. *Redirect Your Focus*
5. *Be Patient...Be Strong*

Once you have read this book, use it as a source to return to when you need it most. Highlight the passages that resonate with you, especially those that have helped you recognize and act upon the changes you have made to put fear into proper perspective. Mark the pages, write in the margins, and write down the quotes and post them where you can see them every day. Remember, *real* change comes through patience, understanding, and *practice*. The changes you seek are possible and, like most things in life, are directly correlated to the amount of time and dedication you are willing to commit in order to achieve your objectives. I believe you will be pleasantly surprised by the results that take place and the happiness you will experience once you begin to act upon these powerful truths.

2

My Story

By Gary Westfal

*"You are far greater than fear.
As soon as you believe it, you will rise to greatness."*
~ Gary Westfal

I grew up in middle-class America with two younger siblings. My mother was a homemaker, and my stepfather was a navy man who was home in between six- and eight-month shipboard cruises. The childhood memories I have can best be described as generally happy with several doses of unpredictability. Truth be told, my stepfather was an alcoholic. When he was sober he was a pretty decent man. I actually have fond memories of doing some neat things with him. He was good with his hands and would teach me how to do practical things, from using the right tools to tying the right knots. I'd help sometimes while he was working on the car or planting a home garden or fishing. He loved to fish and I'd sometimes go with him when I felt confident enough that he wouldn't drink too much and could stay sober enough to drive us home safely.

But there was always an unpredictable nature I had associated with my stepfather. On more than one occasion my mother had to have local law enforcement take him away for the night because he had become physically abusive after inebriation had taken its hold of him. He became a different man than the one I knew in the garden or on the water during a fishing trip. Although I was the oldest, I was still too young to step in and face him down to stop him from physically abusing my mother and terrorizing my younger siblings. Because I was adopted, he would typically avoid taking anything out on me during "the bad times." Then again, I became rather adept at avoiding him. I remember yelling at him as the police led him away in handcuffs one night, telling him not to bother to come back. But sooner, rather than later, he would return with promises to be a better father and husband.

My mother finally summoned the courage to divorce him when I was twelve years old. It was a bittersweet time for me. I was happy he was gone but my heart was torn as I watched my younger brother and sister try to emotionally sort out why he could no longer be part of the family. I had witnessed the devastating effects of fear work its way through my family for years and finally had the satisfaction of watching it physically walk away from what was left of our family unit. We were better off, which was certain. But a new fear had walked in right behind him that I hadn't even noticed—uncertainty. Now what? Mom didn't work. My stepfather was gone. How would we survive? Who would lead the family? I didn't know much about money or income when I was twelve, but I *did* know it was up to me to step up and lead. It was for that moment that I *now* give God the glory for instantly changing my life…although I didn't really fully understand it at the time.

Out of literally nowhere I summoned a boatload of courage and put myself into a family leadership role. I was afraid and had no earthly idea what I was supposed to do, but I knew one thing for sure…I was determined to be the *exact opposite* of my stepfather. To this day I don't care too much for fishing, never work on my own car, and only recently began to see the value in gardens and plants. Psychologists say I *reverse-rolled*, essentially becoming everything *he* wasn't. It resonates with me as I see a measure of truth in the analysis. I'm not perfect, and have actually made several mistakes in my life. But I am not my stepfather's young man, and I'm rather OK with it.

My mother eventually remarried to address her own uncertainty and security needs but there continued to be discord and unhappiness in our family. As the de facto family leader I had a tough time allowing a new man into the house to assume a leadership role and just tolerated him for the sake of making my mother happy. In retrospect I see that it's a tough situation that could have gone much better than it did. I eventually turned to sports and quickly figured out the art of overachievement through hard work and stubborn tenacity. I landed a leadership role as a quarterback on the high school football team and made it my life's mission to be the absolute best I could be until I graduated from high school and joined the air force. The army tried convincing me to "Be All You Can Be," but I saw better options with the air force. No offense, army.

I could write an entire book on the lessons I learned on the football field and in the military, especially in the areas of discipline and dealing with fear. Face a grouchy coach who is tired of losing by a few points for three straight games or a pissed-off drill instructor at three in the morning, and you learn to deal with fear through the regimen of discipline really quickly or you succumb to its wrath.

I enlisted in one of the absolute best career fields in the air force by sheer chance. I was told I would be an air traffic controller based almost entirely on my aptitude entrance examination scores. I had no idea just what the heck an air traffic controller was, but I would not have been as happy and in my own element had I been selected for any other career specialty. It was perfect. I loved to talk, was pretty much beginning to figure out I was a bit meticulous (OK, obsessive-compulsive, actually), and I rather enjoyed leading airplanes around the sky just by telling them what to do and when to do it. To top it off, I was able to see the world, and the US Air Force paid me to experience it all.

It's safe to say I faced my share of fear throughout my life, as I suspect we all have. If there is one lesson that stands out, however, it's that I refused to *ever* allow fear to define me. I am constantly reminded that fear's ultimate *sinister* role is to steal dreams.

Today, one of the most common fears I face invariably surfaces when I prepare to address an audience. *Speaker's anxiety*...ugh! It's the last thing you would expect to learn about me—especially if you know me at all—because of the way I conduct myself in social settings. I'm generally known as someone who connects easily with others, consistently projecting a positive attitude and confident outlook, always smiling. Hey, I like people. Yet when called upon to speak publicly, I have to summon the courage and live by the principles I espouse to effectively deal with this form of fear. The reason *why* was difficult to understand at first. Upon close examination, however, I discovered a stubborn determination for perfection, which I now know to be connected to a fear of personal judgment. The fact that I was able to accurately identify this fear put me in alignment with the first truth: Identify the Fear.

Typically manifested in the form of anxiety, this fear has the power to paralyze progress and crush opportunity, but only *if* we allow it to. To combat this fear, I have trained myself to look beyond the anxiety while living by the truths that mitigate fear, empower courage, and result in a triumphant satisfaction of conquering fearful situations. The good news is that I have learned to recognize this relentless thief and have an effective formula for dealing with it primarily through education, adequate preparation, and the manner in which I mentally frame things.

I believe we can beat fear *every time*. It all starts in the mind. It is fear's battleground, and if we fail to recognize it up front then we are at a disadvantage from the start.

> ***"Every battle is won before it is fought."***
> ~ Sun Tzu

I can still remember the first significant audience I addressed publicly. I was a new adjunct instructor for Embry-Riddle Aeronautical University and had been assigned to teach a graduate class to a small group of students, most of which were active duty air force officers. I had prepared well for the lecture and was excited to have arrived at a point in my life where I could give back to my alma mater.

The class size was small—perfect for a beginning instructor. There were eight students total, and I made a point of socializing with each one before class started—a wise lesson I had learned from a fellow seasoned professor. I kept thinking how neat it was to be able to teach. Then it happened…show time!

As I stood in front of my attentive audience, fear tapped me on the shoulder and introduced itself with a wry smile. I failed to take a deep breath before I began speaking, fumbled with the handouts, and did a pretty poor job of delivering the first half of the lecture. To top it all off, I couldn't help but notice one of the students toward the back of the room who appeared to be about as disengaged as one could be, given the nervous, less-than-stellar lecturing skills delivered by yours truly. Who could blame him, I thought. He was slouched in his chair with his arms folded—a dead giveaway of lack of interest, right?

I approached the student during our first break and asked him what he thought of the lecture. I actually had second thoughts about asking such a question out of fear he would be brutally honest with me and forever negatively affect my teaching career. Instead, his answer both surprised and reassured me. He told me he found the content quite interesting and found my delivery to be "genuine." I smiled and said something about how he *seemed* uninterested from my perspective. He politely apologized and explained that he was a bit tired from flying all day and had made it to class just before start time. I thanked him for his honesty and walked away realizing how easily (and quickly) we can make assumptions that are not always accurate. Note to self: Never allow fear to convince you of the truth, for it is rarely even close and *never* has your best interests in mind.

I'm the kind of person who is intrigued with *why* we do things. In my own self-analysis I discovered how I nearly allowed fear to prevent me from serving as an instructor because of an anxiety associated with public speaking. Why? In this case it was based on perception anxiety. *What will the students think if I say something they don't agree with? What if they simply don't like me? Will my instruction methods be accepted? How will they "perceive" me?* I was so consumed by my assumptions that I actually unwittingly fed my own fears. I also failed to realize how it was never really about *me* at all. As soon as I shifted my focus *away* from me and *onto* the students, everything changed for the better.

Had I allowed fear to pervade and convince me that it was bigger than my ambitions, I would have missed out on so many rewarding and enriching experiences I had as an instructor. Since then I have gone on to speak at several venues and have served several causes, chief among them, my interactions with young adults through mentoring, lecturing, and speaking engagements. The anxiety still occasionally presents itself but I'm now better able to recognize, confront, and handle it.

Years later, when I discovered a love for writing, I embarked on a journey to write my first novel. Writing came as a complete surprise to me late in life but it quickly became a rewarding passion. I had often wondered whether I would ever find my true calling in life, and when writing emerged I knew with certainty that I had indeed found it. I literally discovered the power to write my own story.

It took me a little more than three years to finish my first novel. I had no formal training or mentorship. The only thing I knew to do was…write. So I wrote and wrote, and wrote. I remember writing the first line as clearly as I remember writing the last. Finishing the manuscript was euphoric. In fact, it was one of those moments when I knew exactly where I was, what song was playing in the background, what time of day it was, and how I was feeling. It was the quintessential definition of a true life experience. I had no idea what I was supposed to actually *do* with the manuscript once it was complete, but I had finished. What a sense of accomplishment!

When I was finally able to contain my excitement and compose myself I began the publishing process. I sent letters to about twenty-five agents expecting prompt replies with competing offers for my self-described "spy-fi" thriller. After all, who wouldn't want to represent the next best author to emerge onto the writing scene since Tom Clancy? I kept checking my inbox and postal boxes...nothing. Weeks went by before I decided to write several more agent queries. Then it happened...I received my first rejection letter.

Now, I'm pretty open-minded when it comes to constructive criticism, but I was *not* prepared for a rejection letter from a publishing agent. I felt so...well, rejected! Why is it we are so surprised when fear takes advantage of us during our most vulnerable states? Because that's what fear does. It preys upon circumstance and our (distorted) perception of reality. By the way, I've said it time and again, *things are not always what they seem.* Even *I* have to consistently remind myself of this lesson.

Rejection breeds negativity and self-doubt if we allow it to. Trust me when I say I had my share of self-doubt and anxiety during this time. I began questioning myself, my abilities, and my *calling* to be a writer. To add the proverbial salt to the wound, I received two more rejection letters the following day. What I had thought was a rather harsh dose of reality grew harsher, until I "accidentally" discovered the self-publishing process through a friend.

When I discovered the self-publishing process, I discovered a hope that reinvigorated my determination to publish. Courage and conviction replaced anxiety and uncertainty. My most profound discovery was that my *calling* was alive and well. I was back in the game! In fact, through self-publishing I had more control over the entire publishing process and could literally shape everything from the cover design and interior layout to the release date. I devoured every bit of information I could find on self-publishing, became an expert on it, and eventually published my first novel under my own publishing label. To top it all off, the novel that was rejected several times by traditional publishing agents eventually turned out to be an Amazon.com No. 1 best seller! Go figure.

> **"Things are not always what they seem; the first appearance deceives many; the intelligence of a few perceives what has been carefully hidden."**
> ~ Phaedrus

Anxiety is one of life's most perplexing phenomena, yet, for the most part, there is a pervading peace that comforts and heals once we give ourselves permission to step through the stages of the healing process. Just when we *think* we have exhausted all of our resources…just when we *think* we have tried "everything," something or someone comes along to help show us the way. The biggest lesson here is to not give up. I cannot tell you how many times tenacity has paid off for me. If you want something badly enough there will *always* be a way.

It occurred to me out of the blue one day that any fear or anxiety I have ever faced was pathetically insignificant compared to the liberation and happiness I experienced on the other side of a fearful or troubling situation. Having the courage to step forward in spite of the presence of fear is liberating, empowering, insightful, inspirational, and enlightening. Despite knowing this, however, there are still those situations that present themselves as overwhelming and consuming in which no amount or form of reassurance can be offered to mitigate the anxiety. It is at this point that we must allow ourselves to become temporarily immersed (not consumed) in our situation in order to find the best way out. I often tell people that most all of the answers they seek are already inside of them. All they have to do is discover them and act upon the quiet leading voice of the heart. I compare the process to grieving after the loss of a loved one. Sometimes we need to mentally and emotionally process things before we are ready to take the next step. Just don't forget to *take the next step*.

It has been said that *time heals*. I prefer instead to believe that *time* may be irrelevant and only serves to measure the process by which each of us finds a way out of a given situation. It is the *process* that is relevant and that I encourage you to place your greatest focus on in order to discover the truth that leads to your personal liberation. The process is methodically outlined in this book and can go a long way toward helping you handle fear. It will equally serve in helping you recover from any emotional turmoil you may have encountered because of fear.

Now, let's get to it...

3

The First Truth
Identify the Fear

The ancient Chinese warrior Sun Tzu taught his men the importance of knowing the enemy before engaging them in battle. "For if you know your enemy and know yourself," he wrote, "you need not fear the result of a hundred battles." This early wisdom supports the principle that you cannot expect to fight effectively unless you can identify your enemies, to spot them by their unique characteristics, the warning signs preceding them, and the patterns they typically create.

Early and accurate recognition is the key to gaining an advantage and ultimately an ability to dominate your enemy. The one nugget of wisdom often overlooked in this quote is that of knowing ourselves. As you go through the pages of this book and discover the truths, be aware of the way each truth resonates with you. Pay attention to the still, small voice of personal conviction that is very good at making you aware of the things *you* need to do to effect change. Note the changes your awareness is calling you to make. Your reaction to "the call" will make all the difference in defining the course of your life and the manner in which you deal with fear from this point forward.

The First Truth - Identify the Fear

It is generally believed that fear is not so much a psychological concept as it is an educational one. Although the statement can be debated ad nauseam, it makes sense to admit how difficult it can be to confront something without clearly *knowing* what it is we are up against. Accurate identification leads to awareness. An increase in awareness is essential and is best gained through careful observation and analysis. Awareness is preceded by an open acknowledgement of the existence of fear and provides insight leading to knowledge, confidence, and courage.

An important precursor to identifying our fear is to openly acknowledge its existence. There is no shame in admitting fear exists in our lives. Denying it only adds to the anxiety already imposed by fear and acknowledges fear's power over us. The responsible choice is to admit our vulnerability to a particular fear, openly acknowledge it, and accept the responsibility of effectively addressing it. Only then will we have a fair and accurate assessment of the strengths and vulnerabilities of both sides—theirs and ours.

So, you have a specific fear. Admit it. Acknowledge it. This essential first step can often be liberating to say the least. Failure to get to this fundamental first step will prevent you from escaping the very conditions defined by your fear.

Like most endeavors in life, business, and war, we *must* be able to identify our objective—or, in this case, our assailant—in order to assess its characteristics, its makeup, strengths, and vulnerabilities to effectively exploit and gain control over it. An accurate identification of our specific fear will reveal, more often than not, that our fear is not as menacing as it first appears. We can take comfort in knowing, as a general rule—that *most* things are not typically what they first appear to be.

Great news! Fear is not the *fault* of anyone in particular. Rather, fear exists as a matter of our *reaction* to a set of preconceived circumstances for which we are ultimately responsible. Before you misinterpret this statement, allow it to sink in, and consider a more practical explanation.

Our life experiences are largely determined by the way we react to everything that happens to us or around us, in addition to the choices we make along the way. It means never blaming others for the way we feel, the fears we experience, and the life we lead. By the same token, we should never blame ourselves, because doing so is destructive and counterproductive to the process of overcoming fear and ultimately diminishes our ability to enjoy the nuances of life. It also breeds resentment, turmoil, and frustration.

If you find yourself becoming angry or frustrated with someone as a result of a fearful experience, take it as a clue that you may not be taking personal responsibility to control your *reaction* to it. Fear is not the result of a personality deficiency or fault, so don't assign blame. Doing so displaces the solution focus and reduces your power and ability to deal with fear.

As we attempt to identify our fear, we should be careful to address it with *specificity*. A generic reference to fear does little good to accurately portray its basis, characteristics, or vulnerabilities. Specificity forces us to address fear without misdirection and typically proves to yield the best results in terms of time and exploitation standards.

Part of the identification process compels us to ask tough questions of ourselves in order to determine the source of our fears, which invariably leads us to clarity. The proverbial *childhood experiences* question seems inevitable, and its relevance—among other areas of influence—cannot be overlooked as part of the fundamental aspect of how some of our fears are indeed formed.

- Did you grow up in a fear-filled family, always feeling insecure, never measuring up, and rarely hearing words of affirmation and approval?
- Are you listening to the wrong messages, hearing only what's wrong and how much worse it's going to get?
- What are some of the sources of your anxiety?
- What feeds your fears?

Until you can identify your fears you cannot effectively deal with or expel them. Putting your concerns and fears into words exposes them and enables you to gain power and control over them.

Fear of Acceptance

A young woman I know shops to feel better about herself. She believes the latest pair of designer shoes is just the thing she needs to feel good enough to be accepted by the friends she believes she needs in her life and will allow her to enjoy the social life she envisions.

When the new shoes go unnoticed, failing to meet her expectations, she quickly concedes, isolates herself, and begins searching the refrigerator for something to satisfy her desire to gain control. She overreacts by overeating, thus embarking on a downward spiral of self-destructive behavior leading to further despair. As the night slips away, she ultimately realizes the entire fear-based cycle of self-pity and the manner in which she reacted grew from a simple comparison of what she was wearing to the expectation of others, coupled with a desire to be accepted by people who most likely couldn't care less whether she was decked out in the latest fashion or not.

A belief in our own unworthiness drives us to live fear-based lives. We are afraid of letting people see who we really are, potentially exposing ourselves, so we avoid the one thing that can make us more courageous: vulnerability. Courage and vulnerability are closely aligned and are two qualities that can greatly improve our lives. Vulnerability in this sense exposes the essence of our fears while providing clues about why we fear certain things. If we gain insight into the areas in which we feel most vulnerable, we can begin to determine how we are protecting ourselves. We may actually end up determining that we are overprotecting ourselves with a veil of armor (fear) from what we perceive to be vulnerabilities.

What is your armor? Acceptance? Perfectionism? Cynicism? Control? Isolation?

The fear of acceptance can wreak havoc on our self-esteem and ignite a cascade of self-defeating thoughts that have the potential to take us into all kinds of undesirable places. We must be careful, therefore, not to base our self-worth on the acceptance of others. Instead, we must acknowledge that each and every one of us is unique and possesses qualities that will resonate with some but not others. It is a simple fact of life that some people are unreachable, and acceptance by all is, by most accounts, unrealistic. The good news is there will always be *someone* who will accept us for who we are based on the qualities we possess.

Psychologists tell us that societal acceptance is an integral part of the human experience, while wisdom teaches us that societal echelons or social classes are insignificant to the true meaning and importance of human interaction and personal happiness. Be careful how you make your choices and frame your references because, as we all know, our lives are defined by them.

Our fears are not essentially grounded in what we *believe* them to be but rather in the *results* we connect them to. Our internal struggle with risk and uncertainty play a significant role in this process. For example, I'm afraid of bees, not so much the bee itself but what I believe the bee is connected to—a stinger! In reality, most bees are not inherently aggressive and thus will not likely sting me unless I've done something to agitate a bee or its environment. Yet, my fear of bees is real, or as real as I *perceive* it to be. Upon careful analysis of my fear of bees it occurred to me that I don't *fear* bees at all; I *respect* them. A healthy respect, using fear as a basis of understanding, allows us to remain safe and free from harmful or dangerous situations. The risks and uncertainties are still present; however, I am no longer paralyzed by the distorted perspective of what I had first perceived to be fearful.

We must therefore be diligent in discovering the essence or the *why* behind the fear. Doing so provides us with actionable insight on how to best proceed with a sensible prosecution plan we can effectively manage.

> *"Once you know the why,*
> *the how will begin to reveal itself."*
> ~ G. Westfal

Fear of Public Speaking

For many of us, public speaking can elicit a fear the likes of which is secondary only to a fear of dying. Whether you speak professionally or are preparing to have "the talk" with your kids, your spouse, or your boss, you have no doubt experienced this fear.

So what do we know? We know fear exists and, in this case, is associated with speaking to people. Great start…but we haven't determined a "why" behind the fear. We haven't addressed it with specificity. So, although we have acknowledged that a fear of public speaking exists, a clear and accurate assessment or identification has not yet taken place.

As we begin to take a closer look and identify the nuances of this particular fear, we are able to learn *why* the fear exists. It could be as simple as our own inexperience and preconceptions or as complex as a psychological aversion of some kind. The discovery process allows us to effectively identify the fear and to address its peculiarities to gain progressive control. Simply stated, *knowledge is power*.

Let's assume, in this hypothetical case, the *why* behind the fear of public speaking is tied to a fear of personal judgment. Now we have a *second layer* assessment of fear beginning to reveal its true nature along with its vulnerabilities. Discovery of the *why* behind the fear leads to the *how* in terms of its effect on the individual. Knowing the *why* and the *how* provides valuable insight on the best approach to confront, control, or manage fear.

Knowing the *why* also helps us better assess the *how* in terms of a strategy to employ to adequately address the fundamental elements supporting the basis of our fears. Using the public speaking example, we discovered a fear of personal judgment hiding in the shadow of the broader issue. In doing so we are now able to address, with specificity, one of the fundamental elements of our fear associated with public speaking. This approach falls in line with the natural tendency of our analytical minds to reduce complex problems to a lowest common denominator construct. The methodology allows us to analyze and better understand the underlying fears (at the micro level) helping us comprehend the big picture (the macro level). In essence, we fear public speaking (macro) because we fear being judged (micro).

The micro-level perspective provides insight and places us in a position of power, enabling us to put the pieces back together in a manner that best suits us. This could simply mean we gain immediate control of a specific fear because of newfound insight or we discover new ways in which to handle fear for a given situation or a given time. Either way, we have the fundamental elements of a solution we can link to the other truths.

YOU…Are Always at the Center of Your Fears

It can be so easy to project or displace the cause of our fears onto something or someone else. We often do this because it's difficult for us to imagine how we could actually be responsible for *knowingly* allowing fear into our lives. After all, fear can be so destructive, disruptive, and disorderly.

Would any of us willingly open the door of our homes to a known thief? Of course not. Why, then, would we knowingly allow fear to step in and *rob* us of our dreams, goals, and aspirations? The truth is, most of us wouldn't. Therefore, perhaps the better question is not so much a matter of *why*, but *how*?

The *how* is addressed by our actions through the choices we make. Most of us tend to envision a worst-case scenario first. And it's no wonder, because most of us are conditioned to *expect* the worst, partly because of our conditioning and partly because of our instinct for self-preservation. Therefore, we *choose* the less desirable possibility, essentially openly inviting fear into our personal domain. The dilemma undoubtedly raises the question, *how* can we avoid this?

Choose a Brighter Alternative!

The four-word sentence above may seem overly simplistic or even outright cliché. But what if it were just that simple? After all, the overwhelming truth of choice lies in its powerful simplicity. If the power of choice can bring fear into our personal domain, it only stands to reason the very same power of choice can produce equally profound effects of the opposite nature. Once you realize you will survive the outcome of your decisions—no matter what—your self-esteem is increased immeasurably, and your fears decrease commensurately.

Why is it some people can live a seemingly joyous, carefree life while others seem to be mired in a state of fearful anxiety and woeful existence? The reasons for the differences are often difficult to determine accurately, yet they clearly exist in the behavioral basis of each diametrically opposed group.

While some people live confidently in the present moment or "The Power of Now" as writer Eckhart Tolle eloquently labels it, others are preoccupied with the noise and self-imposed responsibility that they somehow have to be in control of virtually every conceivable aspect of their lives. It's no wonder most people feel overwhelmed when societal pressures place such emphasis on an ability to control the uncontrollable and to attain a state of absolute certainty. Without a clear path to the sources designed to help us confront our fears and strengthen our resolve to overcome the obstacles dissuading and discouraging us, we are simply adrift in despair.

> *"The only certainty in life is that there will most assuredly be uncertainties."*
> ~ G. Westfal

The power of choice and decision making is often severely underestimated. Our choices shape the very course, construct, and condition of our lives. It has been said (and largely believed to be a fundamental truth) that the position we currently occupy in life is personally determined by the sum total of the choices we have made to this very point in time. If you find yourself in a fearful place, perhaps it's time to consider adjusting the choices you make. Remember, *you are always at the center of your fears*. If someone angers you, it is because you have *allowed* them to anger you. If you fear a situation, you have *allowed* (or conditioned) yourself to fear it. Choose instead to understand it and confront it. Once you understand it you must begin to *believe* you can overpower it. And never forget—you can handle it.

The culmination of our perception of fear can best be summarized by our ability to understand and believe that, no matter what, we can handle whatever we believe will happen as a result of a given situation. In other words, as bad as it seems, we are *always* able to handle the situation. To "handle" a situation, by the way, does not infer that we are left on our own. Oftentimes it takes the assistance of others, or at least the awareness that we must enlist the assistance of others, in order to best handle a situation.

Allow me to make an interjection at this point by calling your attention to the fact that it is not implied that we will always be able to *control* the situation, but instead, we are able to *handle* the situation. In fact, it is safe to admit most situations are rarely in the full grasp of our control. Therefore, even if things occur that are out of our control—as with most situations—they are *always* within our ability to *handle*. There should never be a time when we allow fear to ever bring us to the precipice of a total meltdown or suicidal contemplation. Remember, fear is a cowardly thief! It is thin, frail, weak, and pathetic. Break it down, understand it, allow knowledge and understanding to empower you, and you, too, will begin to see this truth as a reality and be empowered to hold dominance over its ruse.

A point of consideration: Why are we so afraid of what other people think?

The fundamental cause of fear is connected to *perception*. In other words, fear's *only* power lies in the power *we* permit it to have based on how we see it. It therefore goes to show that if we can change the way we subconsciously perceive things—especially our fear in its truest form—we can fundamentally begin to change the results we keep getting when we take a step outside our familiar zone. One of the best known ways to increase our strength or personal power is to take a courageous step beyond the limits of our familiar zones. From that point we should embrace every aspect of what we experience as a result of our ability to overcome each instance of fear. To gain power we must concentrate on power. In other words, savor the victory and know we have the ability to survive despite the outcome of our encounter with fear.

> ***"What is behind your eyes holds more power than what is in front of them."***
> ~ Gary Zukav

What will *we* think if we are actually able to achieve whatever we desire? Yes, our very own opinion counts. How will your successful achievements affect your life? Will it affect how you feel about yourself? Absolutely. Will it affect how others see you? You bet it will.

A shift in your perception will allow you to increasingly become known as someone who personifies confidence, happiness, and success because of the way you feel about yourself. Your victory and dominance over fear will begin to precede you as your self-confidence improves. You will be sought after, your relationships will improve, and clarity will increasingly be drawn to you as you become less concerned about specific fears you have had to confront throughout your life.

Stop wasting your time allowing fear to rob you of the power to be happy. Give yourself *permission* to be happy. Yes, you read correctly. You already know *how* to be happy and you know what it takes to *be* happy. All you have to do is to recognize that fear has presented itself as a thief poised to convince you it is not worth the embarrassment, hassle, time, or *failure* you are likely to encounter on the path to happiness, success, and personal victory.

When it comes to success, don't fear hard work. Success comes to those who are willing to do what most others are not. It is that simple. Don't fear missing out on the latest television show or sports season. There will be plenty of other occasions for you to enjoy those things after you reach your goals. Besides, why watch others celebrate their achievements when you can get to work on your own? Are you with me?

Look, there are plenty of people, plans, and programs out there that will show you *how* to succeed. There just are not enough people, plans, programs, and methods showing you how *not* to fail without factoring in the essential element of how to effectively deal with fear.

The following practical exercise answers a common request I often hear when speaking with people in life and in business across the spectrum. Far too many "experts" offer great insight but fall short of providing actionable advice or guidance you can use *right now* to produce encouraging results. My answer is to provide *practical exercises* designed to answer the call for such guidance.

A Practical Exercise to Identify Fear...

Your fear...think about it...visualize it...feel it. Label it. Describe it to yourself. Then...write your description down on paper. Write everything you can and be as descriptive as possible. What emotions does it evoke—in other words, how does it make you feel? Where are you when your fear reveals itself? Is someone with you when this fear presents itself? When is it strongest? When is it weakest?

This practical exercise serves several purposes—one of which is the very act of *identifying* our fears by thinking of them, acknowledging them, and confronting them through the descriptive process—which may be difficult at first—and by purging them through the written process of transference from your mind to paper.

Once you have a clear understanding of your fear, begin by identifying its makeup. What do you call it? What does it look like? Is it menacing or frail? What role does it play in your life? What does it prevent you from doing or achieving? Are you ready to acknowledge your ability to overpower it?

There are several things you can do at this point. Some will advocate simply crumpling the paper and throwing it away or shredding it in a symbolic gesture of eliminating the fear from your life, effectively gaining control over it. Others may suggest you continue to add to it in order to keep it in its rightful place of subjugation. Where you take it from here is up to you. The importance of the exercise lies in its simplicity and the transference from the inner sanctum of your heart and mind, where it is most destructive, to the paper where you can see it. Expose it for everything it is and, more importantly, for everything it is not. These are fundamental steps in the process of understanding fear as it applies to you. Don't worry if you just can't seem to get rid of your fear by doing this exercise. This can take time, practice, and patience because, as I pointed out, it is a process.

Fear of Failure

One of our biggest fears is failure. "What if I fail?" Let's face it; we've heard it time and again—we should *avoid failure* at all costs. The very connotation of the word *failure* elicits a despair or perception that not only instills fear in even the most courageous among us but also implies underachievement, which places us in an "undesirable" societal class. All too often we put these labels on ourselves way before others even notice we have had a "setback."

Fear of failure and our attempts to avoid blame are (all too often) enough of a reason for most of us to do everything we can to avoid exposing ourselves to the *possibility* of success that we miss opportunity altogether. We place such an overwhelming emphasis on our perceived exposure and vulnerabilities to the outside world that we end up accepting the status quo over the exciting and potentially limitless possibilities awaiting us. Examine the true desires of your heart. What is it you want? Step beyond the fear holding you back and grab it!

To quote Felix Dennis, owner and founder of *Maxim* magazine, one of the most successful modern magazines, "... *the nightmare of prospective failure provides you with the very opportunity you are seeking. Not only does it restrain smarter people than yourself from becoming rich—and there can only be so many rich people in the world—it affords you the chance of increasing your confidence, both when you confront it and when you master it.*"

Yikes! I Found Success. Now What?

A friend called me out of the blue when he had heard he had just landed a coveted leadership role as the senior technical director for a US government position he had only dreamed he would ever be qualified to obtain. To understand this story in its full context, you should know that this friend is the closest thing I've seen to what I would call a "born leader." Despite that, however, his accelerated rise late in life had overwhelmed him as his maturity and abilities caught up with him, essentially surprising no one but himself.

It was one of those moments when I remembered exactly where I was when I received the phone call. He called to tell me the great news of his promotion but also to confide in me that he had no clue how he would ever be able to serve in such a coveted position. "People are going to see right through me," he said. "I'll be sitting beside general officers and seasoned fighter pilots helping to make policy."

I patiently listened to him describe a very common fear associated with success—especially a sudden burst or onset of success. That fear, known simply as a lack of confidence, is one of fear's oldest tricks. It shows up on scene when *preparation meets opportunity* and is the destroyer of dreams, goals, aspirations, and happiness.

I wasn't at all surprised he was feeling anxious about his ability to step into the new role; in fact, I'd anticipated it to some extent. I recognized the phone call as a great first step in his acknowledgement of the fear, so I knew he was already on the right track. The fact that he called me to openly discuss it told me he was ready for help in accurately identifying it so he could confront it. As I stated earlier in the book, sometimes we need the help of others to navigate the process of overcoming our fears. Having to ask someone you trust for help should *never* be an excuse or reason to accept fear. Many situations require the assistance of a trusted friend or family member to successfully navigate and eventually escape such circumstances.

When it seemed he had gotten most everything off his chest he paused and then asked me what I thought. After congratulating him I reminded him he already had the seeds of greatness within him. I reminded him of his past accomplishments, both on and off the battlefield. Then I asked him if there would be any difference in anyone else's selection over him for the position. In other words, was there anyone else he thought rightfully deserved to be selected over him? He initially tried defending fear's grasp on his confidence by complimenting other viable candidates. Then I reminded him how his selection was indicative of two things: his abilities and his potential. A very comfortable silence ensued for a few moments as we both felt the presence of truth and wisdom working its way into the conversation while fear took a seat in the corner and confidence began to replace his doubts.

My friend is now a very successful senior technical director at Edwards Air Force Base, California, home of the US Air Force Test Center and the Air Force Materiel Command Center of Excellence for conducting and supporting research and developmental flight test and evaluation of aerospace systems from concept to combat. I'd say he found happiness through his ability to accurately identify the enemy—a lack of confidence—and prosecuted the conditions in his favor. Well done, my friend. Well done indeed.

Instead of *fearing* failure, why not embrace it? Think about it; failure sometimes happens. It comes about as a result of an oversight, misperception, procrastination, or myriad other reasons and causes—some well within the confines of our control, some not so much. Most often, failure is a result of our inattention to detail or inadvertent missteps on the methodical path we most likely *should* have taken to achieve a desired objective. But for some reason, we simply didn't. In other words, most times failure is avoidable and our choices often have something to do with it. But, for various reasons, we still fail. Our typical first reaction—a normal one by the way—is one of despair and self-deprecation.

If you're like most people, you simply dislike the word *failure*. Here's a universal truth…and you'll know it as such by whether or not it resonates with you…

> *"A failure can only remain a failure if you choose <u>not</u> to learn from it."*
> ~ G. Westfal

If you permit a failure to permanently reside in the win column, the failure will dominate your life and negatively affect your choices going forward. However, if you draw upon the lessons of failure, it'll *transform* your life in amazingly positive ways. The failure becomes an *opportunity* to learn, improve, and enhance your life. So, although despair is a normal initial reaction, don't get stuck there. Instead, summon whatever emotion or initiative you have to move forward with a new *educated* perspective. The new perspective should be one that carries forward only the *lessons* of failure and not the failure itself.

We often spend so much time and effort planning to avoid failure that we neglect to take action because of the uncertainty we have of our ability to totally eliminate the *pos-*

sibility of failure. We don't fully account for the value failure brings. Yes, failure has *inherent* value.

What are *your* fears? Intimacy, inadequacy, relationships, rejection, success, heights, public speaking, confrontation, poverty, personal security, dying, uncertainty, failure itself… some or any of these? All too often the premise of our fear isn't something we can physically grasp or manipulate. We fear beginnings and endings inasmuch as we fear the status quo. And it is precisely because we cannot physically manipulate our fears that we become frustrated and preoccupied with trying to *avoid* our fears altogether instead of identifying them and confronting them head-on.

Afraid of the Dark?

I was talking with the mother of two young girls who are fearful of the dark. We were discussing the generic concept of fear when it occurred to me that I had not yet addressed this fundamental fear in terms she, or more importantly, her daughters, could comprehend. The focus of our conversation resonated with me as I, too, grew up fearing the dark, which is not uncommon among most children and even more common than most of us realize among some adults. The descriptions of the experiences her daughters faced could've easily been applied to my own childhood encounters. So it is my contention that those of us who have experienced this fear may share similarities in how we perceive what we cannot see. In this case, that which we cannot see is literally…*everything*.

The similarity of our fears does little in terms of providing an actual remedy to those who experience this type of fear. It does, however, provide a sense of empathy to those of us who have successfully overcome them, thereby lending to a better overall understanding and a more accurate diagnosis.

The value of empathy and effective diagnosis provides insight into symptoms associated with the fear of darkness. It also lends itself to viable solutions that may help to overcome our fear of the dangers we perceive are awaiting us in the dark. As for identifying this fear; well, that's the easy part. If you have it, you certainly know it. As for our children, if they fear the dark, they will let us know in a number of ways and will not likely reveal it to us subtly. There is more on how best to handle this common fear in the next chapters. The first step is recognition and admission. If you or your children are afraid of the dark there is nothing to be embarrassed about. It is one of the most common fears known to man. So, if it affects you, you're normal. The fact that we know we are afraid of the dark is a victory, albeit one providing little consolation beyond the knowing or identification of our fear. But this step is nonetheless significant if we are to get past this or any other fear for that matter.

To recap this first truth…we have the *what*, the *why*, and the *how* leading us to a better understanding of our fears in terms of proper and specific identification. We have also learned we are able to handle the ensuing results of virtually any situation through the power of choice. We are now armed

with the knowledge it takes to proceed to the next step...
Confrontation!

Some Helpful Advice...

Don't move on to the next truth until you have clearly identified your fear. The next truth requires you to engage with your (known) fear. In other words, you will face your fear and address it accordingly. If you don't know or lack a clear understanding of whom or what you are confronting, it complicates the process and will only lead to inevitable frustration. It is akin to confronting a thief without a weapon. It is senseless to do such a thing. So, spend the time necessary to adequately fortify yourself with the knowledge to identify your fears and then move through the next truth with confidence and an assurance that you will ultimately find the answers you are seeking.

4

The Second Truth
Confront the Fear

Once we've clearly identified our fear, we must confront it. This can be one of the most "fearful" aspects of overcoming fear. Most of us have been taught to avoid confrontation at all costs. After all, confrontations can be so…messy. It's true, confrontations can cause tensions to rise, but it doesn't have to get messy at all. In fact, effective confrontation can be liberating and lead to several good things—knowledge, wisdom, improved relationships, psychological and emotional relief, and personal growth (confidence) among them.

Aristotle believed courage to be the most important of virtues "because it makes all others possible." Today, we can most assuredly agree that courage is one of the most neglected and troublesomely deficient areas of human psychology. As research (and interest) in this area grows, however, we have begun to better understand the nuances of courage and how we can cultivate the ability to face our fears with greater fortitude through courage.

If you think about it, most of us fear being judged. We are so afraid of the personal assessment of one another that the mere possibility or idea of being analyzed in *any* capacity can induce a concoction of physical and emotional reactions of paralytic proportions. Just the thought of a confrontation can be enough to cause us to find any number of ways to avoid the angst that we forget the reward lying just beyond the veil of deception cast by many of our fears. In fact, personal judgment is by far one of the most feared aspects of human interactions aside from rejection, whether we are interacting with one person or one hundred. Its basis is so closely connected to rejection that we see judgment as a precursor to *outright* rejection and a threat to our basic survival instinct of belonging. After all, we are social beings by nature.

More often than not, we misjudge or overreact to what others *may* be thinking in terms of our performance, appearance, intellect, abilities, value, or unique personal traits that we begin to believe our own presumptions. These overreactions and miscues can actually prevent us from realizing a goal, objective, relationship, or opportunity. It may even impede our ability to overcome an emotion that would otherwise bring about positive personal change and empowerment or healing. For example, if we are avoiding a new relationship or life experience because of a painful reminder from our past, we must first confront the lingering elements that reveal themselves as a fearful basis or contributing factor.

What most often weighs us down and brings us the most misery is our memories or perceptions of the past. We hang on to past hurts, past experiences, past failures, and become consumed by what *was* rather than by what *is*. The reflective process, in this case, is one that repressively rules our lives and controls our perception of reality.

One of the first things we must do is release all resentments. After all, what good does it serve to continue hanging on to the hurt or hatred? As we evaluate the circumstances of our past relationships we must be careful to consider every conceivable element, to include our own contribution to their demise. We must also be mindful of how our fear of self-exposure will affect a new relationship or life experience. This fundamental process requires an honest acceptance of the past event or initial cause of the fear and an acknowledgement that the past is only relevant unto itself. The only inherent value remaining lies with the lessons it provides to *improve* current and future relationships and experiences.

When it comes to relationships, most of us fear repeating the same mistakes. And, unless we take a good look at ourselves from the inside out and conduct an honest self-assessment of how we may have contributed to the relationship or its demise, we set ourselves up for a repeat experience. In other words, as difficult as it may be to admit, the full "blame" of the entirety of the issue does not always lie at the feet of others. Like it or not, we play a role—at least to some extent—in the function of relationships and *always* have a choice to concede to the basis of our fears or the integrity of our beliefs and values.

A commonly overlooked aspect of confrontation is the process of interacting with ourselves, effectively taking an accounting of just what it is *we* fear and then facing—or confronting—those fears. This process of *introspection* can be equally as difficult as a *physical* confrontation because of the emotions it may force us to face.

The Courage to Try

Confrontation takes courage. The very thought of being courageous implies there is a factor or presence of risk, which is generally a true statement. However, we are reminded that where there is no risk there is no new understanding, no healing, and no transformation.

Courage comes by way of understanding the nuances of the fear you are confronting. Courage is a necessary element to have at your side when confronting fear because it will carry you through any resistance you may experience as you step forward to face fear. Confrontation is the one step in the entire process of conquering fear that is the deciding factor in determining whether or not we can move forward. Some of us fear confrontation more than fear itself and unwisely choose instead to accept the status quo because of the aversion we have to this essential, but intimidating, step. Don't be that person. Keep reading to find out how you can free yourself to discover new horizons that will take you *beyond* your fears.

Courage is a state of mind we must adopt in order to best effect the process of confrontation. In this sense, the proper and most appropriate definition of courage is not one supported by arrogance but rather by confidence and knowledge. True confidence is gained through knowledge of the truth.

The truth is, most of the resistance you will experience will *appear* more menacing than it actually is, while other forms will be bona fide obstacles you must effectively and systematically deal with in order to move forward. If you should encounter an experience of inevitable blowback or defensive resistance—more commonly to be expected when confronting others—don't avoid it, don't contribute to it, and don't concede to it. Instead, look for ways to isolate it and remove it from the central point of focus. There's always a way. After all, it's just another obstacle posing as a thief, appearing more menacing than it truly is. Conquer it and you will be the victor and well on your way to the progressive solutions you seek.

Keep in mind that any defensive resistance you may experience from others typically stems from their own fears. When faced with no other alternative but to confront someone, do so by first attempting to understand as much about a person as possible. The time you take in doing so will help the confrontation process go a lot better than it would have otherwise. Ask yourself some basic questions before the confrontation process:

- "What will the other person likely fear in this confrontation?"
- "How will he or she react?"

"How can I mitigate his or her fears in order to conduct a mutually beneficial conversation rather than have a full-blown confrontation?"

Go into a confrontation with the mind-set that your reason for being there is not personal. Do your best to keep the topic of conversation focused on the issue and not the personalities behind the issue. Remaining focused on the topic will have its own natural effect on personalities without having to openly define or identify them.

> *"I learned that courage was not the absence of fear, but the triumph over it."*
> ~ Nelson Mandela

A few years back I had a robbery in my home...*while I was home.* I was writing in my office in the back of the house as it happened. I was unaware and later discovered I had been robbed after the thief took a few items, including my wallet. The thief quickly escaped through an unlocked front door never to be seen or heard from again. I never had to confront the thief, but had I been faced with that situation, I would have had to take a stand to protect the sanctity of my home. Would I have been scared? You bet. My life may have depended on how I handled the situation. It plays over in my mind to this day and has changed the perspective of my awareness. And I'm better prepared because of it. My role was, and is to this day, to be the defender of my domain. It can therefore serve as an analogy to every other fear we have. For you too are the defenders of *your* domain and should *never* allow fear to rob you of the experiences that are rightfully yours to enjoy.

Stop Resisting Who You Really Are.

Many of us have a *crystal-clear* image of who we want to become and what we want to achieve, yet some of us *fear* becoming *exactly* what we envision. Why is that? Quite simply, we fear everything associated with the things we cannot clearly see or accurately predict. We allow fear to dominate the "what ifs" surrounding the very possibility of our successes. And because of its deception, we give in to our fear and become convinced we are somehow not worthy or good enough to possess that version of ourselves. What a tragedy.

By taking action to realign ourselves with who we are meant to be—our talents (we all have them), our tendencies, our beliefs, morals, values, and our passions—we better prepare ourselves for our intended purpose: our success and happiness. We also mitigate inevitable fears. Notice, once again, it is not insinuated that we will always "eliminate" fear, because fear is a stubborn phenomenon that, like the thief it is, will show up when we least expect it. It will show up when we are least prepared. So, to quote the American Boy Scout motto, "*Be prepared.*" Sounds simple enough, right? Well, quite often, it's the simplest truths that bring about the most profound changes.

How many of us have watched the mannerisms displayed by a successful person and wondered why they seem to operate with such ease and attract the trappings of success? It all seems so easy for them. They display enviable confidence and are generally happy and well liked. When they speak, people actually listen to them. What is it about them that sets them apart from others?

For starters, rarely, if ever, is it easy. And rarely can individual success ever be narrowed down to one elemental difference. But a common trait among most successful people will undoubtedly reveal a conviction or an underlying courage allowing them to confront their fears in order to protect the sanctity of their dreams, goals, and objectives. So where do these folks find this seemingly elusive courage? They develop it just like you will as you discover the truth and go through the steps outlined in this book.

Let's face it: The very nature of fear requires us to operate with courage if we are to stand up to its ruse and effectively deal with its intended undesirable effects. As you know, courage doesn't just appear out of thin air when we summon it. We have to *build* courage by understanding our fears as well as the nature of the very thing we fear. So we come back around to the first point of effective identification—the *what*, *why*, and *how*. Only then can we begin to build courage by getting to know our fears, why we are afraid, and how best to manage our fear.

It may offer some peace of mind for you to know that some 90 percent of the things we worry about in our lives never materialize. So, in essence, the negative worries of uncertainty we allow to consume so much of our time, attention, and consternation have a less than 10 percent chance of being accurate, much less even materializing in the first place. Like the great pretender it is, fear operates from a statistical disadvantage yet continues to stake the untenable claim of restrictive influence we allow it to possess. The short lesson here is that our time can be much better served focusing on the positive aspects of our lives. Instead of worrying about what *may* happen, why not enjoy what *is* happening around you *right now*. In other words, savor the moment. After all, it's all we've got.

As we get to know the essence of our fears, we begin to see things differently. The renewed perspective will most assuredly reveal our fears, empowering us to *act courageously* while we step into the confrontation process with confidence. The essential element in this step is action that allows us to transition from a place of fear and uncertainty to a position of power.

Fear and uncertainty cause weakness, be it physical or psychological. The analogy, and hence the point, is the same. Weakness *empowers* fear whereas power (and courage) enables us to gain an upper hand on the process of understanding, eventually reducing our fear. It is therefore essential for us to operate from a position of power if we are to effectively handle fear. So how do we do that?

Communication in All Forms Is an Essential Element of Relating with One Another.

In order to confront or conquer anything, we must take *action*, but not indiscriminate action. If we are to effectively incapacitate the enemy (fear), we should be as precise as possible. In so doing, we reduce the effect fear has on us while we begin to gain control and grow personally.

So, fearful situations, confrontations among them, can actually *enhance* the quality of our lives once the experience of the encounter is behind us and we have taken the lessons forward. But the only way to get beyond them is to push through the process of confrontation. As you confront the darkness in your life, think of the process as a rite of passage to the ensuing truths leading to conquering this fear and increasing confidence and courage. You cannot skip this step. It simply doesn't work that way.

Most of us have heard the old adage "when you fall off a horse, you should get right back on again." Although the *origin* of the cliché is somewhat elusive and irrelevant, its substance and intent is *highly* relevant. The phrase supports the premise that if something traumatic happens to us, we should step right back into the very situation as quickly as possible to prevent ourselves from developing a fear of it. It is the essence of how fears are created if we otherwise accept the experience as reality and fail to confront, validate, or reengage.

For example, many people swear off relationships after a failed marriage or bad breakup. This is unfortunate because the lessons of life are missed if the wisdom gained from such circumstances is ignored or set aside. The value of wisdom to a new relationship cannot be understated. The real trick is to be sure to carry forward only the positive wisdom gained and not the baggage that led to its demise. And so it goes with the manifestation of virtually *any* fearful or otherwise unpleasant encounter. We must be aware of how we process our experiences and our encounters while being careful to consider how to categorize them correctly for the overall betterment of our lives.

The process of reengagement as a way to address our fear is powerful. There's nothing more liberating than to find out that our fearful assumptions were inaccurate. The simple truth is that some fears will be evident (or preconceived) until we confront them. There may be trace elements remaining even *after* we've completed the confrontation process. After all, it *is* a process. But the process becomes easier over time with your ever-increasing courage, knowledge, and personal power.

It's a Process, Not an Event...

The confrontation process can take many forms. Some confrontations are intrinsic and require deep personal introspection, acknowledgment, or admission, while others may require personal or physical interaction or an overt expression—forgiveness or acceptance for example—in order to overcome fears. The following are a few points to ponder as you seek the courage to confront your fears. Consider them as you think about your own personal circumstances.

- **Is your fear keeping you from moving forward?** If so, then a confrontation is in order. If your fear has you under its thumb, frozen by the uncertainties of life, it is essential you face your fear and begin to effectively deal with it if you are to remove it from your life. Do not neglect to include the essential first step of accurately identifying your fear and the circumstantial nuances that feed it.
- **What's keeping you here?** Do your fears have you fooled into thinking it is just easier to accept them or delay them for a more appropriate time? Well, *easy* is not always best. In fact, if you conduct an honest assessment of what is keeping you "here" instead of moving ahead with the desires of your heart, then you should easily be able to discover reasons to confront your fears and summon the courage necessary to propel you onward to action, progress, and achievement. Delay satisfies an immediate urge to find solace, but in the long run the choice *not* to engage traps you in the very state you despise—a fearful one.

Sometimes courage will first manifest itself through simple intolerance. The sentiment of becoming sick and tired of being sick and tired may be all you need to summon the courage to face your fears and begin to see them for what they truly are. If you have reached this stage, then be careful not to overreact. Instead, allow the intolerance to be the beginning of your personal journey to overcoming your fear.

➤ **Apathy is one of the most destructive tactics in fear's arsenal.** Don't give in to the highly convincing argument that apathy is OK. Apathy is defined as a lack of interest, enthusiasm, or concern. These are danger signs pointing to an acceptance, rather than a repudiation of your fears. Don't buy into the notion that you have to accept the restrictions imposed on you by your fears. You *do* have a choice.

Apathy has become an epidemic in global communities as we are continually bombarded with sources of stimulation that step in to ease the burden of having to face our fears. Apathy strips us of the power of choice through a process of overstimulation. These sources of stimulation trap the masses in a never-ending cycle of comfort and familiarity, essentially robbing them of any ability to continue to move toward goals, dreams, and desires.

If apathy is your issue, then it could be that you are merely operating outside the lane of your intended purpose. A lack of enthusiasm is an indicator of lack of interest. The first step in combating apathy is to ensure your dreams, goals, and aspirations are in line with your true desires or purpose. To help provide a level of insight, consider your answers to some of the following basic questions.

- Am I happy?
- Am I loved?

- Do I belong here (in this relationship, job, city, etc.)?
- What is my purpose?

> **Withholding forgiveness is holding you back more than you may believe.** Are your efforts to find success and happiness continually met with frustration? Is your heart heavy for some unknown reason? Do you truly believe you are *worthy* of success, love, happiness, prosperity, and joy? Are you frustrated that you just cannot seem to figure out why everyone else seems to be getting ahead while you cannot? Taking the time to conduct an honest assessment of our innermost selves—an introspection—can pay huge dividends in terms of revealing areas we need to address personally to effect change. Resentment is typically at the heart of non-forgiveness and envy. Remove resentment and you're well on your way to getting past emotional anchors that are holding you back more than you realize. While you are at it, trade your expectations for appreciation and your whole life will change.

Is your fear real? For that matter, is your desire real? A lot can be learned through the process of confrontation. Just as fears are exposed, so, too, is the dedication we have to the cause for which we are committed. The process of confrontation can be as simple as a discovery of the truth or as complicated as an encounter exposing personal vulnerabilities and opportunities to improve, which are equally beneficial for healing and growth to take place. What is really lurking in the darkness? Is it exposed when the light is turned on? If it disappears, then this fear can be eliminated because the light has exposed its ruse. If it is revealed, then celebrate the victory of being able to clearly identify the fear (the first step in the process).

You may have heard that confrontation is as much an art form as it is a technique. It is true that to engage in a confrontation of any sort requires some familiarization with the rules of the game. Therefore, it is important to keep in mind some of these considerations when confronting your fears.

Prepare to Be Humble and Be Prepared to Rumble

The process of confrontation often requires a bit of humility. We must see ourselves as human beings, complete with all of our imperfections and misperceptions as we enter the confrontation phase. This manner of thought gives us an advantage to see all sides of the issue and adequately prepares us to humbly accept the changes we must personally make to facilitate the process. Confrontation, although typically an offensive move, doesn't have to be offensive at all. Coupled with a real sense of humility, empathy, and compassion, a lot of insight can be gained from taking action to confront our fears.

Just as the confrontation process requires a measure of humility, so, too, does it take a measure of courage. While some confrontations can be relatively easy, others may come with a dose of resistance in the form of "blowback," especially if you're dealing with an individual or group. As I pointed out earlier, it is wise for you to keep in mind that any resistance you experience may be based on someone else's fears. How's *that* for a contrasting consideration? Whatever the reason, don't fear the resistance because, like most good things in life, your ability to power through it will reward you handsomely on the other side. Just remember to remain issue-centric by keeping personalities on the sidelines.

Begin to take control of your life through the confidence and power of your increasing courage. Confronting your fears is a vital step in the process of understanding and effectively addressing the nuances of fear. Although not always a pleasant experience, effective navigation of the confrontation process allows us to experience the positive results of being able to get back on course to the life we desire and rightfully deserve. Successfully navigating the confrontation process places us squarely on the path to strength, fulfillment, and happiness. Each step we take away from our familiar zone is a step toward the empowerment of those ideals.

A Word on Trust...

When it comes to trust, we should be careful to place the power where it rightfully belongs—in the palms of our very own hands. We must trust ourselves first and foremost by believing we have the ability to handle the things that come before us at any given time. Only then can we begin to trust the foundational truths contained in this book with respect to handling our fears. Trust builds confidence, which builds courage, and so begins a successful journey in building upon the sound truths helping us better understand—and confront—our fears.

While you are contemplating what you have read so far, consider the following story of a man who faced his fears while confronting several discouraging obstacles in one of the most demanding, complicated, and stressful career environments.

5

Blood, Sweat, and Fear
A Story by Scott Duke

"To embrace fear is to overcome it."
~ Scott Duke

Most job surveys identify air traffic control among the most stressful jobs in America. You see, air traffic control is an occupation in which every decision made must be right, every time, all the time. Rarely is there a second chance to get it right. The fear of failure or even the slightest error in judgment is always present, as it should be in a profession in which the slightest error can potentially result in catastrophe and loss of life.

I have been an air traffic controller for more than four decades. You might think having a fear of failure would be an *odd* fear for a professional whose responsibility it is to safely guide people across the nation's skies. On average, air traffic controllers will have more lives in their hands in *one day* than a surgeon will in a year. They will communicate with pilots, fellow controllers, and a host of other agencies nearly nonstop from the time they "plug-in" and begin orchestrating the skies until they hand over the responsibility to another controller in this nonstop, chaotically organized world of air transportation.

In high school in Kentucky, I was always the class clown, and I had the grades to prove it. It was my steadfast belief that getting a laugh from my fellow students was far better than any grade I would get for the class I was attending. And if I could pull off a smirk, grin, or a laugh from my teacher, well, it would be like a George Costanza (from the TV show *Seinfeld*) moment: "I'm out!" Of course on the flip side was my ever-present fear of hearing no laughter at all and suffering the consequences of that.

When I graduated high school (some would tell you I was socially promoted rather than actually graduating), I joined the US Air Force at the age of seventeen. My recruiter quickly learned how much I liked to talk and suggested I become an air traffic controller. I thought I knew everything back then. I had assumed I knew pretty much what I was in for with this air traffic control thing, so I jumped at the opportunity by accepting the most excellent career field choice from the recruiter. I figured I'd show them how smart I was by being ahead of their game. I went straight to the library the next day and found a book on "airplane hand signals," memorized all the signs, and was ready to be an air traffic controller. What puzzled me was why the air traffic control school was scheduled to be twenty weeks long. There were not that many hand signals and I had already learned them all, so what could take so long?

When I attended military basic training I was given a formal briefing *accurately* describing my Air Force Specialty (air traffic control). My heart sank to my stomach as I actually listened to the details of the job description. *Good grief,* I thought. I am going to be responsible for the *expeditious flow of air traffic*? What in the world does *that* mean? I was going to be responsible for people's lives? Hey, wait just a minute! No one ever mentioned anything about *hand signals.* The fear of failure had tapped me on the shoulder and introduced itself with a wry smile. Suddenly, I knew I should have taken high school a bit more seriously.

I attended the air traffic control course at Keesler Air Force Base, in Mississippi, at the famed Cody Hall, which was an iconic facility full of history for all air traffic controllers stretching back to the Vietnam era. Cody Hall was the place where ordinary air force airmen were turned into extraordinary air traffic controllers…well, sort of. For me, the path was bumpy, as the twenty-week course turned out to being closer to *forty*. I was "recycled" in nearly every block of instruction, and when I failed the Federal Aviation Administration exam for the second time I was escorted to the superintendent's office. It was there that a "seasoned" chief master sergeant, who had more time in the bathroom than I had in air traffic control, warned me that I would be changing tires at the motor pool if I didn't pass the exam. It was my *last* shot.

The fear of failing something as significant as a major exam can be a life-changing event. It was nearly overwhelming. For the first time in my life, charm, a quick wit, and a sense of humor were not going to be enough to get me a good grade on that exam. For perhaps the first time I can ever recall, failure was not an option. I had suddenly discovered a resolve to overcome fear if by nothing more than sheer will…and a little hard work. I had to buckle down and try this thing they call *learning*.

I waited for what seemed like hours for the exam results to be released and posted on *the board*. The wait was agonizing. Then it happened. The exam results were posted. I had *soared* past the minimum passing score…by a whopping three points. Relief washed over me as the fear of failure literally evaporated. I felt a real sense of pride…until I realized this was only Block One! There were *five* more blocks of instruction to go. Instantly, the fear of failure returned as if it had never left. It goes without saying that if you attend a twenty-week course and it takes *forty* weeks to graduate, the fear of failure will likely follow you like a ghost on assignment to spook the heck out of you the entire way.

While in Block Three—training in the control tower and the control tower lab—the unwritten policy was that any violation of an air traffic control rule causing an aircraft accident resulted in having to take the "crashed" model aircraft with you everywhere while on breaks. The problem with that was that nearly all the student breaks occurred at the same time, so twenty-five to fifty fellow students in the course bore witness to you standing there with your model airplane. And every one of them knew you were directly responsible for allowing an aircraft to crash. On one very bad day in the lab, I managed to violate so many rules the instructors made me take the entire airport layout (a four-foot-by-eight-foot wooden construction model of an airfield) to the break area! To say I was a bit uncomfortable would be an understatement. Oh, how I longed for the use of those hand signals I had memorized.

Doom and Gloom...Not so Fast!

My sense of impending failure grew stronger as the days wore on and I continued to fall behind. My confidence had sunken to an all-time low as I watched my former classmates graduate and get their assignments to various air force locations around the globe. Things got even worse when I entered Block Six. This final block of instruction was the most intense, most dreaded, and most feared by all—the *radar* block. Darkened rooms, quiet whispers into headsets, and radar scopes marked with intimidating lights, switches, and dials, each with coded blocks of data on the radar displays that I actually had to understand and use to separate aircraft from one another.

This final block of instruction, while an indicator to most that we were nearing graduation, was, for me, a fear *multiplier*. Completion of this block was considered a rite of passage, but was complicated with so many rules, regulations, and procedures it was often difficult to see past the obstacle of my fear of imminent failure. To prove our mettle we had to actually *demonstrate* our understanding by applying everything we had learned. Radar standards are so different from those we learned in the control tower. We had to learn to think three-dimensionally while looking at a two-dimensional radar screen. We had to learn how to use a technical style of thinking to separate aircraft vertically, longitudinally, and horizontally.

While working in the radar lab in my final block of training, I made some key errors that resulted in the simulated collision of two aircraft. One of the aircraft was piloted by a single person while the other was a larger aircraft with fifteen people on board, including the pilot and co-pilot. The instructor pulled me out of position and directed me that my homework for the night was to write condolence letters to each of the families explaining how my mistake cost their family member his/her life. Brutal…

As I ultimately made progress through this last arduous block of training, a secondary fear began to emerge. I began thinking about actually graduating and going to an air force base where those aircraft models and simulated radar targets would suddenly become *real* airplanes with *real* people flying them. I could not begin to imagine how being a class clown was going to get me out of this mess.

My fears about being an air traffic controller had reach their highest point and were nearly overwhelming, but I managed to pass the final block if only through sheer tenacity, an ever-increasing *aptitude*, and an enduring positive *attitude*. When I heard the news that I had passed the course I made a mad dash to the assignments board to see where I was going next. My eyes followed the line across the paper to the base assignment section when I had found my name. It simply read "Campbell AAF." *What the heck was that? AAF?* I wondered. I asked one of the instructors for help (at this point, I knew them all) and he told me A-A-F stood for *Army Airfield*. Good gracious! I knew I wasn't the *best* student at Cody Hall, but was I so bad the air force decided *not* to send me to an actual air force base and instead ship me over to the army? Just when my fear had reached its highest point, I was now mired in despair.

When I arrived at Fort Campbell I quickly learned that the number of aircraft operations that occurred here (especially helicopters, since this was the home of the 101st Airborne Division, the "Screaming Eagles") ranked the control tower as one of the busiest. *Good grief, what have I gotten myself into*, I wondered.

I was relieved when I walked into the office and saw blue air force uniforms. Whew! I was at *least* surrounded by folks on the same team, but the fear of being able to actually perform as an air traffic controller in a live environment was still at the forefront of my mind. Fear had successfully placed doubt in my path as I continually questioned whether or not I could actually do this job. If my technical training was any indication, I was *not* going to fare well in the great state of Kentucky. Despite having passed the basic course, fear had given me every reason to question my ability to perform. But I courageously stepped forward and ultimately earned my first air traffic control certification by the grace of God and the assistance of some very good trainers.

My fear of stepping up to the mic and controlling air traffic eventually diminished. Notice I said *diminished*. The fear never really goes away. It *does* become insignificant over time as we gain an upper hand through competence, practice, and understanding, which produces an underlying confidence. I gained the confidence I lacked. I also gained the competence that is an absolute imperative for an air traffic controller. To date, my list of accomplishments in this illustrious career field includes the attainment of fourteen control tower certifications, six certifications in radar facilities, an Associate of Science degree in Air Traffic Control and Instructional Technology, and a Bachelor of Science degree in education. In fact, I was so grateful for the training I received during the air traffic control course, I later volunteered to return and serve as an instructor.

In 1991, I deployed in support of Operation Desert Storm and was selected to serve as the radar chief controller at Al Dhafra Air Base, United Arab Emirates. Trust me: if being an air traffic controller in a combat environment doesn't invoke some kind of fear in a person, he is probably in total denial and in need of clinical or psychological intervention of some kind.

As I write this, just a few months shy of retiring from air traffic control altogether, I look back at a 41-year career with a confident nod at the fears I faced. I overcame them all through a process that includes some luck, a lot of fortitude, a stubborn will to keep my dreams and goals alive, and ah yes, a sense of humor I never truly let go of, as I became what I had set out to become—an air traffic controller!

Today, I work at the National Guard Bureau in Washington, DC, and serve as the oversight authority for all air traffic control in the Air National Guard. Me, of all people…go figure! Yes, I went from class clown to learning hand signals to being the Chief, Air Traffic Control, Airspace & Ranges Division. Now if that doesn't put fear in perspective, nothing will!

~ Scott Duke

6

Conquer the Darkness

Darkness is a physical manifestation of the unknown.
~ Gary Westfal

We are visual creatures by nature; therefore, we tend to fill the empty space in our lives with what we perceive should rightfully occupy that space. In so doing, our overactive imaginations "help" us prepare for a worst-case scenario when we are confronted with the absence of light in both a literal and figurative sense. Some clinicians tell us our fear of the dark is a good thing as it is a defense mechanism derived from years of evolutionary self-preservation. But fear can outlive its usefulness if it begins to interfere with things like healthy sleep patterns and the normal functions of life if it escalates to a point of phobia.

Because we are deprived of one of the most essential senses (sight) at night, we rely more on other senses and become acutely aware of things like noises. Add to this the typical silence nighttime brings and we have the elements that are sure to lay the groundwork for an anxious environment, especially to those of us with active imaginations (artists, writers, children, musicians, analysts, etc.).

A Practical Exercise in Confronting the Dark…

Darkness equates to uncertainty, which can lead to anxiety and an outright fear of what we cannot see. Whether yours is a legitimate fear of the dark in a practical sense or a fear of the darkness of the unknown in a philosophical or figurative sense, the confrontation process compels us to evaluate our perceptions. So how do we do that?

Take a moment to look around you. Then, close your eyes. What do you see? Nothing, correct? The inability to see with your eyes closed is no different than being surrounded by darkness. Why then do we feel there *is* a difference? The answer lies in how we have programmed our minds to believe a difference exists. We tell ourselves a dark room is "different" than simply closing our eyes. Yet, in both circumstances there is an absence of light. I believe if you ask anyone who is blind whether a difference exists you will understand the clear difference of perspectives in personal programming. Think about this simple exercise as you read the following sections on this aspect of fear.

Literal Darkness

A significant point to remember with respect to our fear of the dark is that it is not the darkness we fear inasmuch as it is the perceived or imagined dangers concealed by the darkness. The things we are exposed to play a large role in how we form our perceptions. It is a fact that most crimes, especially burglary, assault, or rape, take place under the cover of darkness. The movies we watch (and allow our children to watch) play upon our senses while confirming our fears when they portray fearful images and scenarios, most of which happen under a cloak of darkness.

Children are said to have some of the most creative imaginations. It therefore goes to prove their fear of the dark is deeply rooted in what they *don't* know or have yet to learn. Their ability to distinguish fact from fiction is a literal work in progress. The basis of their fears, therefore, is limited to what they know and what they imagine, the entirety of which is not limited to the elements of happiness and security. Parents can play a *significant* role in reducing the fearful imaginations of children by regulating one aspect of visual stimulation—television—among other things they are likely to see and hear that tend to feed their fear.

The best thing a parent can do when dealing with a child who has a fear of the dark is to communicate with them in a loving and calm manner. Reassure them that you understand and will take measures to help them through the process. The good news is a child's fear of the dark is typically temporary and can be significantly reduced by the compassionate understanding and reassurance of a loving parent. Compassion and empathy will do more to lessen this fear than most any other method or tactic. As parents we must remember that, while the monsters may not be real, the fear is *very* real.

If your fear of the dark brings demons, danger, and doom to your mind then your mind will begin to consider darkness as the dwelling place for these imaginary elements. Every encounter with darkness will bring fear, anxiety, and uncertainty to the forefront and will control this aspect of your life… unless you take steps to change the perspective. Consider the alternative in which a dark room can become a place of quiet solitude, an escape from the noise and distractions of life, a place where you go to meditate or pray and find true introspection and the quiet leading of wisdom. What a powerful example of the mind-set of perspective.

Figurative Darkness

Fear of the dark manifests in many forms. While most of us have experienced literal darkness, there are those of us who have also encountered figurative darkness. Figurative darkness is deeply personal and can present itself in the form of isolation, depression, loneliness, rejection, confusion, and despair.

Good news! Figurative darkness can be overcome. While this type of darkness can appear during some of the most difficult periods of our lives, it is *typically* temporary. The nature of the word *temporary*, however is contingent upon your desire and action to escape the bonds of its allure. Yes, figurative darkness, although extreme, can become a familiar place of diametric comfort. In other words, as bad as it is to remain in figurative darkness, there are those who fear the transition of escape and the liberation of breaking free from figurative darkness more than they fear figurative darkness itself. Depression and loneliness, for example, can be a "safer" place than the unknown of what lies just beyond the bounds of figurative darkness. CAUTION: Figurative darkness is powerful and has the potential to entrap you long term if you *choose* to relinquish your personal power to it.

There are both clinical and practical approaches to dealing with figurative darkness. If yours is a seemingly insurmountable darkness that cannot be overcome by practical methods, you are encouraged to seek a clinical solution. Rest assured however, there are solutions with either approach. The point of the message is to take *action* to step out of the darkness and into the light of a new chapter of your life.

> *"Your actions will produce an alteration of the circumstances that surround you."*
> ~ G. Westfal

How Are You Framing Your References?

Perspective is everything when it comes to addressing fear. Assigning an accurate perspective to our fear presents an opportunity for us to gain a tactical advantage, thereby allowing us to effectively confront it. The manner in which we initially frame our fear sets the circumstances of whether we will be able to find solutions to overcome the fear or accept it as a reality in defeat.

For example, instead of framing fear as "an issue," try instead to label it as "an opportunity." The positive spin empowers us to believe we can handle the circumstances and find an effective solution. The same can be said of just about any other area of your life and the manner in which you communicate to yourself. Try replacing "I hope" with "I will," "one day" with "now," "I wish" with "I am," and watch the conditions of your life transform as your confidence increases and your ability to confront your fears with conviction and assurance soars.

Keep an Open Mind…or Rather, Open Your Mind

A simple change in the way we communicate can make a profound difference in many areas of our lives. Communication is expressed in two basic forms: internal and external.

Internal communication, or the manner in which we communicate to ourselves, is so very important and literally shapes and defines the way we think and the manner in which we speak and act externally. Our internal communication is a culmination of the emotions, desires, experiences, and stressors we allow to occupy our minds. Both forms of communication contribute to the dominant emotion we ultimately select as the driving force of our lives and is overtly displayed to others by the way we present ourselves externally.

External communication is primarily driven by our internal programming. However, it is important to note that it is our external choices that feed our programming. Therefore, we are wise to guard against faulty or destructive input to ensure the best possible internal programming of our minds.

An entire book can be written on this aspect of our psychological makeup. The purpose of this passage, however, is to provide insight on something we can choose from two entirely different options yielding extraordinarily different results. We can reshape the way we communicate to ourselves, and ultimately to the world, by first adopting a positive attitude.

Positive thinking isn't a new concept, yet few people fully understand the effect it has on the balance of our lives. I think we can agree that the manner in which we communicate is driven in large part by the basis from which we think, as mentioned earlier. If we are positive minded, our outlook tends to be just that—more positive. If we are more cynical and generally negative minded, our outlook tends to reflect those attributes. The good news is we can reprogram ourselves to accept a more positive mind-set with some practice and continuous exposure to programs (and people) that will help us.

A positive attitude alone is not enough to confront our fear, but it is an absolutely essential element to have in the overall quest to overcome our fears. There is an inherent power in optimism. Successful people we wish to emulate have a common trait of enthusiasm formed principally on a positive outlook. Their joy drives them. They attract positive things into their lives using the rules governed by the *law of attraction* and avoid negativity and cynicism. Call it karma or the universal law of nature or whatever you wish, but we all see it and desire it. If it works for them, why shouldn't it work for us? So if a positive attitude is such a great attribute, how do we go about developing one?

A Practical Exercise in Developing a Positive Attitude...

The following quote helps us start this exercise off with the right mind-set...

> *"No one can make you feel inferior without your consent."*
> ~ Eleanor Roosevelt

Here are some things for you to consider doing as you step into a positive state of being (mind, body, and spirit). Practice these things and you will be well on your way to the ultimate representation of a positive attitude—happiness.

➢ **Use your filter.** Your consent or permission is required for you to perceive anything. In other words, you are solely responsible for deciding whether to accept or reject anything you witness, read, or hear. The fact that we are free to accept or reject these things implies an inherent power we all possess. So, always remember: You are powerful. *You* make the decisions that will ultimately affect your life and, as a result, you will always be able to handle the outcome because…you are powerful. The sooner you believe this the sooner you will begin to see your power materialize.

- **Think before you react.** You may not be in control of a *situation*, but you are always in control of your *reaction* to it. If you can create your own misery, it only stands to reason you can create your own joy. How you react to an event is as important as, if not even more important than, the event itself. You are in charge of your reactions, decisions, choices, and responses—all of which form the basis of your perspective and ensuing circumstances. Until you fully realize and accept that you are responsible, you will fall short of achieving full control of your life. Unless you're incarcerated, you retain full control of the decisions you make, so choose wisely.

- **Stay balanced.** When we are confronted by fearful situations our minds tend to become imbalanced. We must be mindful to consciously step away from the chaos and fog of uncertainty in order to reestablish balance and harmony. Armed with the knowledge that we are powerful and in control of our reaction to life's situations, we can begin to see how we can effectively *choose* to be positive inasmuch as we can *choose* to be otherwise. Statements such as "You make me angry" or "That hurts my feelings" or "I just can't seem to get a break" can be changed through the power of choice. Changing our thoughts *instantly* changes what we attract into our lives and immediately affects our reactions and our attitude. If you are easily angered or your feelings get hurt by what others say, make a choice *not* to be affected by them. Too simple? Don't overcomplicate it, because as you will ultimately realize, simplicity lies at the foundation of most solutions.

At this point, you may be thinking, "Easy for you to say, but my situation is (different, unique, complicated, etc.)." To that I'd say *you're right*. However, while your situation or circumstance may, in fact, be difficult, different, or unique, it is not immune to the principles of personal responsibility and choice. In fact, you should never compare yourself to others in this or any other manner.

➢ **Stay fit.** We can talk all we want about the importance of a healthy mind-set, but if we are not physically healthy it can present an incomplete formula to being 100 percent in sync with a positive state of mind. Regular exercise and a healthy, balanced diet go a long way toward reducing the stresses and strains of life. Don't neglect to make this a vital part of your complete success formula. Eating well and exercising consistently pays huge dividends that go far beyond the obvious.

- **Define your own life.** Using other people as role models is one thing we are taught in order to duplicate the effects of a successful outcome or endeavor. But to *compare* your life to others to defend your circumstances is nothing short of an excuse. It is absolutely unacceptable and can, in fact, be self-destructive because our minds inevitably begin to draw contrasts reminding us more of inferiority than of our own self-worth and unique value. Therefore, proceed with caution and instead, seek opportunities to become *more* through the lens of your own introspection. In other words, define life on your own terms.
- **Be present.** If you are like most people, your view of the world is centered on and around *you*. We create our reality by the things that happen to us or around us, but that's an incomplete picture. By expanding our perspective on how life affects the whole—everyone, everything—we gain wise insight and a wider glimpse of reality. Only then can we begin to accurately shape our inner selves by the reality of our outer world. We must first be mindful of the present moment. In doing so, we effectively gain an appreciation of the true nuances of life. Details begin to emerge, changing our perspective from a self-centered construct to one revealing how we fit into the entirety of life. As a result, patience and perceptions are enhanced, happiness and joy emerges, and fear is alleviated.

> **Smile!** A smile is contagious and often returned, but we must take action by first projecting our joy and happiness to others. Happiness is a state of being. It is a precursor to projecting a positive outlook. It is difficult to project a positive attitude if we are unhappy. So, find ways to be happy. There are plenty of things to be happy about. Even the smallest things can bring joy to our heart and a smile to our face. If we are genuinely happy we can share our happiness openly and honestly with others through the exchange of a smile. Who knows, your smile may be a difference-maker in bringing light to the life of another through this simple but meaningful gesture.

A positive attitude goes a long way in helping to guard against fear. Your positive attitude is a coat of armor and a first line of defense against fear's tactics.

Entirely too many of us have become used to the way things are. We accept the status quo simply because "that's the way it's always been." Every one of us possesses the power to dream. The tragic truth is many of us have given up on our dreams simply because of fearful preprogramming. We begin to buy into the belief that perhaps we don't truly deserve to get ahead or be forgiven or achieve peace, love, or success. After all, most everyone else has the same fears and they're not doing much about it, so why should we?

Instead, if we will open our minds to the idea that each and every one of us *deserves* to find peace, harmony, and happiness in some form, we will begin to become encouraged with the knowledge that fear is not as menacing as it seems. At the very least, fear is not worth yielding to at the expense of our dreams and peace of mind. The old adage of "be careful because you just might learn something" applies here.

The following are some suggestions to help you get on the path to a positive mental attitude and to support a healthy maintenance plan as you reprogram your subconscious away from a fear-based perspective in pursuit of your goals...

- **Your computer:** There are so many electronic resources available to us today that can be just the thing you need to see how others are living their lives supported by a positive way of thinking. YouTube and a host of other websites contain a near endless library of topics from simple positive messages to in-depth analyses on virtually any topic of interest. These resources can be accessed easily and are powerful tools in the arsenal of your success support options. Connect with electronic resources that educate you, inspire you, and empower you with the insight and the seeds of change. A simple Google search can reveal countless resources of inspirational quotes, methods, and blogs, all designed to feed your desire for a refreshing perspective to your outlook. Consider connecting with me on my biweekly blog, Introspection: www.gwestfal.blogspot.com, or visit my author page on Facebook: G. Gary Westfal - Speaker, Writer.

- **Audio programs:** Part of the shift in the way we approach things has a lot to do with our programming. In order to make a change, we must *reprogram* ourselves. One of the best methods of reprogramming is through the use of audio programs. You will be pleasantly surprised by how fast a commute to work can be while listening to a good positive audio program. I have found myself sitting in the parking lot on occasion just to finish a segment before heading in to the office. The positive difference it can make in the tempo of your day is noticeable and contagious.
- **Live seminars:** There is nothing like the energy of a live seminar to convince you of the power of a positive outlook. If you have ever been to a concert, a Broadway play, or have had the opportunity to listen to a live personal coach or motivator speak, you know what I mean. If you have not, you owe it to yourself to attend at least one live event during your lifetime. You will leave with an inexplicable sense of enrichment and maybe even a dose of confidence or wisdom that will awaken something powerful within you, putting you on course to recharge your outlook and change your life.
- **Books:** Books are great tools to add to the arsenal of your positive thinking maintenance plan. I recommend you purchase books and consider them as your field manuals and vital reference sources. Purchasing as opposed to borrowing convinces your subconscious

that you have taken ownership and consider these vital tools a permanent part of who you intend to become. Highlight them, make notations in the margins, and put one in every room of the house. If you are serious about making significant, positive changes, you will have no issues with doing the little things that will make big differences in your life.

- **Quotes:** Inspiration comes in many forms. One of the most profound forms comes to us through the simple wisdom of a quote. If something resonates with you, write it down and place it somewhere you can see it on a daily basis. The more you see it, the more your subconscious is convinced of your new state of mind.
- **Affirmations:** Declarative statements made by you as being currently true are strong ways to bring about rapid changes in your life. Our subconscious minds do not distinguish fact from fiction and are easily convinced based on what we say and how we act. How many times have you experienced a change in emotion just by watching a movie, listening to music, or reading a book? While our conscious minds are fully aware that we are witnessing or experiencing something totally fictional, it does little to keep our emotional reactions from rising and falling at the pace and plot of the narrative in which we are involved, even from a safe distance. This reaction is quite simply your subconscious at work.

Your affirmations are an important part of convincing your subconscious to believe what you want it to believe even if it is not yet a reality. When forming your own affirmations, remember to state them as if they currently exist and keep them positively based. You must feel as if you own these statements, so it's important for you to write or say them in your own way or style. Otherwise, your subconscious will know and will resist your honest efforts. The one element that will overcome the tendency of your subconscious mind to resist is a crystal clear vision or mental image of your goals and desires. And the one way to create goals and desires is with passion and conviction. You deserve it, so *believe* it and it shall be!

Some examples…

- "I am happy, healthy, wealthy, and wise."
- "I am attractive, pleasant, and have a lot to offer in a relationship."
- "I'm worth every penny of an increase in my salary."
- "I am well-prepared; therefore, success flows to me freely."
- "Knowledge and wisdom are drawn to me because my mind is an open door to their counsel."
- "Drive and motivation are at my side continuously."
- "My body is healthy and my mind is sharp."
- "I am a success in every conceivable way."
- "I am perceptive and see opportunity everywhere."

There are some who don't believe in affirmations as a source of convincing power to the subconscious. If that describes you then perhaps an alternative approach can be found with *incantations*. Incantations, traditionally defined, are a form of magical spell cast upon something or someone. Bear with me as I attempt to navigate ever so gracefully around the whole "magical spell" part of the definition and go right to the "command" aspect. You see, our subconscious minds respond to two fundamental stimuli—that which we perceive as reality and that which we *command* it to adopt.

There will be times when we must command our subconscious to adopt the reality we wish or hope for because we firmly believe in it and we know it to have inherent value to our lives. Admittedly, there is something magical taking place when we use this technique to address our subconscious mind.

A command convinces a stubborn subconscious mind by using an authoritative *emotion* to begin believing in the reality of things that have not yet occurred. *Convicting* emotions should always accompany incantations because our conscious (rational) minds have already processed our desires and are waiting only upon the subconscious mind to be convinced to produce the reality we seek. Emotions evoke a serious (and convincing) overtone to commands, thereby drawing a clear distinction between incantations and affirmations. Incantations can be highly useful in this sense and have been known to noticeably change lives, most especially when our subconscious mind requires a "good swift kick" to convince it to get on board with our objectives.

Some examples...

- "I *command* my subconscious to..."
- "...break free from this destructive relationship."
- "...bring forth the wisdom with which I have programed myself."
- "...be articulate, convey purpose, passion, and meaning to my audience."
- "...help me find the answers to questions I seek."
- "...attract the right person into my life."
- "...bring creativity and prosperity into my life."
- "...show me the path to happiness."

What You Say Is as Important as the Manner in Which You Say It

The thoughts we dwell upon and the words we speak define our reality. It is a magnificently designed formula we can use to take control of the course of our life. Too many people simply miss this profound truth.

Controlling our inner voice can sometimes be a difficult task to accomplish. Fear's closest ally—doubt—is typically the first to show up on scene when we are faced with an unfamiliar situation or brand-new opportunity. Doubt is largely to blame for the negative or discouraging tone of our inner voice. That tone, if not checked and immediately corrected, has a tendency to quickly manifest itself in the words we speak and messages we convey.

You may be intimately familiar with doubt. It is a cowardly culprit that is all too eager to remind you how unworthy or undeserving you are to enjoy new experiences or opportunities. Caution! Once you give doubt any credence whatsoever it will stop at nothing to convince you of the inherent fear lying just beyond the attraction of your desire. Recognize doubt for what it is—an accomplice to fear. Face it with courage. Use the conviction of your desire for change and the positive experiences of life to defend yourself against its deceit.

How many times have you been around negative-minded people? Do they project power or weakness? Do they draw others in or repel them with the attitude of their words and the energy of their demeanor? Choose your words, thoughts, and mannerisms carefully. Positive proclamations, along with the right questions designed to find successful, genuine outcomes are important aspects of effective confrontation. So, too, is the manner in which your statements are delivered and your thoughts are framed. Support your statements and questions with a positive attitude and operate with an expectancy that a solution *will* result. It is not as cosmic as it sounds. In fact, it is a universally accepted truth that…

"The world…and the power of your thoughts… will bring you exactly what you declare."
~ G. Westfal

The story in the next chapter captures the essence of how one woman faced her fear of loss, having endured her own sense of darkness. Her story serves as a reminder to us all that darkness *can* be overcome. Her determination to savor the nuances of life, despite her circumstances, are defined by the manner in which she frames her experiences. Through her heartfelt words she reminds us of the fragility of life and describes the prescriptive power of quiet introspection and grateful reflection to overcome.

7

Butterflies, Birds, and Blossoms
A Story by Jan Waddy

> *"Life often presents us with fearsome turmoil.*
> *We can allow fear to define us—or refine us; the choice is ours."*
> ~ Jan Waddy

We both loved nature's blessings. Frequently, Larry would elevate his wheelchair to its highest level and watch as I refilled the hummingbird feeder just outside the bedroom window. It would take just seconds before the tiny creatures would dive-bomb each other in a torpedo whir of green, red, and brown to get at the nectar.

We'd also planted a butterfly bush and blooming plants in the backyard to attract the "flutterbys"—a term we adopted for butterflies after hearing it in a performance by Ossie Davis and Ruby Dee. We'd sit and watch the iridescent spicebushes and the swallowtails stop to feed. As we sipped coffee, they floated in and out of the yard. Larry "captured" many of the birds, butterflies, and blossoms with his camera, and for my birthday last year, he gave me a beautiful stained-glass butterfly. It remained in its carton because I didn't remember to ask for help in hanging it until after he was in the hospital. On one of her visits, our daughter Ruth Maria and I hung it in the front window. "Now, it will be the first thing Dad sees when he gets home," I said as we admired it from outside.

After four surgeries on his back that eventually put him in a wheelchair, the chances this time were better than any of the others. We were both anxious about the surgery, but the alternatives were not good either. The top of Larry's spine was closing and he was unable to grasp things and had stopped doing the things he enjoyed because his hands and arms had gotten so weak. Without the surgery, he would eventually be paralyzed from his neck down.

He agreed with the doctor. The surgery to relieve the stenosis in the neck (with a 95 percent chance of going well) would take a few hours; he would spend time in rehab and then return home with his hands working and the weakness in his arms gone. He would get back to his jewelry making and photography, which he loved and did so well.

The surgery itself went well, but the following morning, things changed. Larry was suddenly gasping for air. He couldn't breathe. The team of nurses and doctors hurried in and intubated him. He was transported to another hospital closer to our home to make visiting easier. What was once our dream of success had suddenly turned into a nightmare.

Over the next few weeks he developed double pneumonia and his kidneys were beginning to fail. He was transferred to a long-term acute care hospital. The doctors were not optimistic. Larry was on a ventilator and hooked up to IVs providing him nourishment and meds. Still, I refused to give up hope and prayed daily for a miracle.

On May 13, Larry went into cardiac arrest and had to be resuscitated. A day later, his heart failed again and he was once again resuscitated. Fear had grown into a knot that now lodged itself somewhere between my heart and my throat. Driving back home that evening, I prayed. Doubt and trepidation kept gnawing at my insides. Sleep and hunger evaded me. Questions plagued me. Was it fair for me to want Larry to live in a vegetative state? (The doctor's diagnosis had been explicit.) I did not want Larry to die. Was my not wanting to let him go based on selfishness? How would I manage without him? I didn't even want to broach the idea, so my prayers were a litany of pleadings for strength, miracles, and answers as to what I should do.

The doctors asked me to sign a *do not resuscitate* order because any further attempts would cause Larry more pain and would just prolong the inevitable. Now fear gripped my heart with a stranglehold and was establishing firm roots as I paced back and forth just inside the entrance to the ICU. Our youngest and oldest sons were there with me, and fear was evident on their faces as well. Our daughter was on her way, coming in from Austin, Texas, while our second son was scheduled to arrive with his family from out of state.

My heart was breaking for my children. I tried to hide my own fear for their sake, but we were all caught like insects in a spider's web. I believe fear does that. It renders you paralyzed—unable to function, unable to think clearly, unable to see beyond the moment. I knew I had to try to be brave.

After speaking with all four of the children, we agreed to sign the order under the condition that the prescribed rules for intensive care be waived and I would be allowed to spend the night or stay during the day without having to leave every two hours for an hour of "time out." The doctors agreed. I thought it a cruel compromise because it meant I had to admit my husband was indeed dying.

At some point I made my way back to the house to shower and change clothes. I remember praying so hard and so loud asking for a reprieve. As I turned the car onto our street a large Caracara flew overhead, and I suddenly felt a sense of calm and peace. I knew in that moment that no matter what happened, God would always be near. I could carry on.

Larry died on the morning of May 16 surrounded by his family. It was a beautiful day. The dawn had broken and the birds outside his window were singing. We cried and prayed and said goodbye.

Arriving back at the house, I immediately noticed a petunia plant, which had voluntarily appeared beneath a rose bush about a week and a half earlier. Now it was in full bloom, a burst of bright red flowers. I smiled, somehow knowing there was a message in the petals that my dear husband was all right.

The next day, as I sat on the patio having coffee in the backyard, a beautiful swallowtail butterfly came to say good morning. It floated for a while then drifted away. The phone I had taken outside with me rang. It was our daughter. As we talked, I turned suddenly and gasped an astonished "Oh!" On the other end, Ruth Maria said, "What's wrong, Mom?"

"Nothing is wrong, sweetheart. It's the orchid cactus. It has two of the most beautiful blooms I've ever seen." The orchid cactus, with its long scalloped appendages, is beautiful sans blooms, but this one—on this particular morning—chose to display a striking show of brilliant red petals and vibrant yellow stamen. I customarily have coffee in the yard in the morning and take notice of the plants as they begin to bloom, but I had not noticed that this plant even had buds on it.

The week after Larry's funeral, with the thought of working through the grief weighing heavily on my heart, I'd made plans to attend our grandson's baseball game, the second one in the tournament for that day. The problem was, I didn't know where they were playing. I called his maternal grandmother because I knew she would be there. She gave me the directions first and then said, "Jan, I have to tell you what I'm seeing here. There's this black butterfly just hovering over home plate. It's so pretty and it just reminds me of Larry."

I got to the ballpark a good twenty minutes later and squeezed in next to her just as the second round of the tournament began. My grandson came up to bat, and there was the butterfly just above him. I gasped another "Oh!" I thought I might just be imagining things, but to my mind, the butterflies, the birds, and the blossoms were happening too often to be coincidence.

All summer long, each time I went to the cemetery, a hummingbird would come to visit along with a few butterflies. A mockingbird stood watch in a barren tree and always sang the sweetest melodies. This happened until the summer turned to fall.

In July, my sister who lives in California invited me to go along with her and her daughter's family to visit our siblings in Louisiana and Mississippi. She knows me well and sensed it would be good for me. She was right.

The visit to our sister in Mississippi found me in her backyard admiring the herb garden she was so proud of. An enormous swallowtail slowly winged its way into view. Two of my sisters came outside and were astonished at the size of the butterfly. By this time I was getting used to hearing myself say, "Oh!"

The day we left Louisiana, a black and red butterfly made an appearance at the passenger side of our vehicle. My niece, who was sitting in the front passenger seat, was already convinced having heard the butterfly stories thus far. She simply said, "Hello, Uncle Larry," as we turned the corner heading for the highway.

Well into November, long after its cousins had migrated south, a Rufus hummingbird visited at the feeder. I watched it from Larry's favorite spot at the window. The little russet-colored visitor would hover at the window, looking me squarely in the eye before going to the feeder. It was more than special.

Since Larry's death, there hasn't been a single day when something at our home has not bloomed. Even as I write, the Lady of Guadalupe rose bush is in full bloom, two of the five African violets are showing their different shades of purple, and right next to the computer where I sit, the orchid, which was a gift for Larry's funeral, has buds, a first for that particular plant. Ironically, it is just below the stained-glass butterfly.

Now, some readers will think all of this is coincidence or that I simply had not noticed these things happening before. Perhaps so, but I choose to believe otherwise. When I am at my lowest points, I am most aware of the gracious gifts God provides for us. I have many "Oh!" moments. And one thing is most certain. All these things I have experienced have erased the fear and replaced it with an increased awareness and appreciation of the bountiful blessings we all have the opportunity in life to enjoy.

I know now each time I see a butterfly, a hummingbird, or a blossom, I will think of Larry and know in my heart of hearts that love provides a spiritual connection the grave can never destroy.

— Jan Waddy

8

The Third Truth
Replace the Fear

Once you have experienced the excitement and euphoria of successfully confronting your fears, you will be empowered with a newfound conviction propelling you toward your dreams, goals, and desires with confidence. You will also undoubtedly experience a noticeable absence or reduction in your stress levels. This is the perfect time to take specific actions that support and reinforce behaviors and beliefs. Your actions will ensure that fear remains in its rightful place of subordination. This chapter will help you see the importance of replacing your fear with empowering thoughts and actions. You will also learn specific steps to take that reinforce your ability to operate above fear. You will discover the benefits of commitment in doing everything it takes to replace your fear with the insight and courage you have gained from the identification and confrontation processes.

I learned early in life that the combined value of knowledge and wisdom can create a formidable force and an undeniable foundation of confidence in the war against fear, not to mention the benefits extending into many other areas of life. In fact, *confidence* is the summation of knowledge and wisdom combined. Think about it: Knowledge provides insight to the *unknown*—the elements we are most afraid of. The accumulation of knowledge helps us to increase our wisdom in order to see what we initially perceive to be fearful and, in essence, reveals fear for what it truly is. Only when we see something in its truest light can we most effectively deal with it.

Fear Replaced by Knowledge/Wisdom = Confidence!

Confidence precedes a person. Confidence—not arrogance—renders a certain amount of credibility and evokes an attraction. Confidence is the combination of certainty and preparedness, outwardly expressed. Why *wouldn't* that be attractive? Certainty stems from knowing something as a truth, a fact, or a revelation, which leads to wisdom or personal enlightenment.

To replace our fear with confidence, we must strive to gain knowledge by taking the time to understand fear in its elemental construct. Whatever it is you fear, begin by breaking it down in order to help your mind realize how everything is comprised of basic individual elements that, by themselves, pose no threat whatsoever. This exercise essentially reduces an otherwise menacing deception presenting itself to rob us of our goals and aspirations, experiences, and ultimately, our success and happiness. The exercise also transforms our perspective in such a way that quite often decreases the overwhelming appearance of our initial perceptions. In other words, wisdom essentially shows us how things are never as bad as they may initially seem.

I read and hear a lot about the fear of public speaking. Standing in front of an audience is said to be one of our greatest fears. But there are actions a speaker can take to lessen the effects of fear and ultimately replace fear. For example, if it is the audience you're concerned about, try to mingle with the group beforehand if at all possible. Learn everything you can about your audience—their philosophy, their demographic, etc. If you don't have time to mingle, don't sweat it. Most of what you should know about your audience should have been provided by the person or group who initially invited you to speak. Begin your speech with a story relevant to your topic. Your insight and efforts will most assuredly elicit a positive response or will have an effect of changing the energy of the room that will, in turn, drive your confidence to the next level. Above all, remember the audience does *not* want to see you fail. After all, why would *anyone* take the time to attend a speech given by someone they expect to fail?

Make direct eye contact with your audience during your presentation and resolve to bring an energy level commensurate with the subject matter. Audiences respond more to energy, enthusiasm, and tone of voice than to content. Just make sure your content is relevant and you are prepared to present it. Your familiarity with your material is by far the best way to reduce anxiety and boost your self-confidence enough to ward off any fears or concerns you may have.

For more information on how to manage the fear of public speaking, please refer to the excerpt from *Overcoming Fear*, provided at the end of this book, by my friend and fellow author Larry Waddy.

Adjust Your Frame of Reference

If your fears lie elsewhere, try to gain a different perspective than what is considered ordinary or customary. Afraid to fly? Find out if you can arrange to sit in the cockpit of an aircraft on the ground and speak with a pilot about flight safety. Oftentimes, an increase in knowledge or a change in perspective is all it takes to affect or lessen fear. Afraid of the dark or the unknown? Your fear resides inside the confines of perception. Seek to gain the truth or reality concerning these fears.

I recently returned from a vacation in Roatán, Honduras, where I encountered Caribbean reef sharks while scuba diving. Now, I'm about as fearful of sharks as anyone can be if I'm on *top* of the water swimming or snorkeling. However, if I am below the surface diving *with* sharks I'm not as fearful. I attribute the difference to a simple philosophy of perspective. As a diver, I have a wider perspective of the shark's natural environment and can effectively keep an eye on its movements and react to any behavioral changes. The difference in perspective provides an alternate point of view that effectively *increases* my comfort level while *reducing* anxieties or fears that would otherwise exist if I were at the surface. It also enhances the positive aspects of the experience and increases my courage, albeit to a respectable limit with these amazing creatures.

It is certain to me that, on some deeper level, I'm fully aware there really is nothing to fear. Yet, fear is a stark reality that exists nonetheless. Therefore, it is wise to understand fear *will* be present in some fashion as we continue to grow. Growth occurs when we step into something new—a new job, a new relationship, and just about any new situation we can imagine. New situations are inherently unfamiliar or unknown. It is the unknown factor that is largely responsible for most of the fears we experience.

Redirecting our focus from *avoiding* fear to *anticipating* a positive experience *through* fear ultimately leads to personal growth. Think about it: When we are motivated to push past the ordinary into the extraordinary in *spite* of our fears, more often than not, we gain a sense of confidence as we experience the euphoria of accomplishment, positive feedback, understanding, and personal victories, just to name a few of the benefits. We literally *feel* the process of growth as we gain perspective, experience, wisdom, and confidence.

Each step we take builds upon the previous and helps us to move out of our comfort zone. One of the most difficult tasks to accomplish is to step outside of our comfort zone. It's just not…well, comfortable. It's not *comfortable* because it's not *familiar*. Unfamiliar things tend to look quite ominous at first.

The very thought of doing something new is enough to intimidate even the most courageous among us. But even the slightest step toward your desires will lead to noticeable changes, to include the way you perceive your fears. It is up to you, however, to *notice* the changes and to celebrate them. And when you do notice them, you will be empowered to go beyond *accepting* change and begin to embrace it instead. Take action in the form of a small bold step into the face of your fear and watch the conditions of your life transform. Do something every day that widens the scope of your comfort zone. Even if your actions don't produce the intended results, you have exercised an act of courage inevitably expanding your comfort zone. You will experience the satisfaction of personal growth through personal power because you have elected to act courageously.

Action Produces Change!

Most of us are *victims* of our own experiences or of the personal conditioning that forms the basis of our fears. Each experience has created a perception of how we believe a given situation will play out. So...

Don't Be a Victim; Instead Be the Victor!

There is a universally accepted truth describing an often misunderstood philosophy that allows us to have, be, do, or experience anything in life we desire. All we have to do is call it into our lives and act upon its leading. Some refer to this truth as the *law of attraction*. Some call it divine governance. Others simply refer to it as the manner in which our thoughts, choices, and decisions manifest themselves. Call it what you wish. After all, I did note that it is a universally accepted truth. The amazing thing about this philosophy lies in its simplicity and the fact that it works.

The premise of this truth supports the notion that "like attracts like," so as you begin to change you will notice how you will begin to attract things into your life, helping you become the kind of person you desire. The old adage of *seek and you shall find* applies here.

Declare your victory as you begin to experience positive changes in your life. In other words, tell someone. And never ever discount your victories as something that would have most likely happened anyway. Be grateful and be quick to recognize how *you* can bring goodness into your life simply by the manner in which you begin to perceive things and the manner in which you react to them. Verbal declarations are among the easiest to manage and have the greatest effect on helping us expand the boundaries of our familiar zone. Each step beyond the zone of familiarity reveals an insight we don't currently possess. A declaration is a powerful statement to both the world and to our subconscious of our intention to embrace the changes taking place in our life, no matter how fearful they may first appear to be. Vocabulary improves our ability to express ourselves and reduces our frustrations. It also has a tendency to increases our self-confidence, which reduces our fears and projects a personal power that others begin to take positive notice of.

Instead of declaring hope, declare victory. Using words and phrases such as, "I wish," "I hope," or "I can't" implies we have little to no power over our life. Begin *today* by enacting declarations of power over weakness. Instead of declaring a dream, draft a plan. Instead of acknowledging obstacles, visualize solutions and accomplishments. These simple declaration exercises invigorate the soul and convince the subconscious to pursue the reality we seek. The result is one that builds strength and personal power that *will* bring about real change and will have profound and lasting effects upon your life.

Most books written on the topic of success neglect to consider how, as humans, we generally fear change, which is the very thing that accompanies a desire to succeed. Change is not always easy; that we can agree upon. The reality, however, is that life is a series of never-ending changes. Whether we like it or not, change will affect each and every one of us throughout our lifetimes.

Some will claim they have no issue accepting change and yet are very often the ones who wonder why their lives remain caught in a perpetual cycle of stagnation as they reluctantly deal with change. While these people claim to accept change, effectively *reacting* to it, others *embrace* change, seeking ways to incorporate it with an objective to gain the most from it. While one group *fears* change the other group anticipates it. The manner in which it is handled can be a difference maker in terms of whether or not opportunities for change—and success—are easily recognized. After all...

Most opportunities lie just beyond the veil of individual perceptions and attitudes.

A Practical Exercise on *Replacing* Your Fear...

- **Replace your fear with knowledge.** *The unknown* is fear's best tactic to deceive you with a distorted reality. Once you buy into the deception of the unknown you will succumb to fear and will limit your ability to move past it with any significance. However, if you spend the time to gain clarity, you will begin to see fear's vulnerabilities. So how do we gain clarity?
- **Read, watch, and listen.** Knowledge is generally defined as an awareness or familiarity gained by exposure and experience of a fact or situation. In other words, we gain knowledge by taking action to feed our minds in whatever way possible, either through familiarity (education) or practical experience. We read, we watch, and we listen to relevant sources of information that enlighten and inform. We take action and fail or succeed based upon our "experience" and learn accordingly by the terms of either outcome.
- **Seek wisdom.** Knowledge precedes wisdom. Wisdom is gained by the *experiences* we have that are the result

of the knowledge we gain. Wisdom increases our overall acuity and insight for truth, which ultimately culminates in an increase in courage, confidence, and clarity.

- **Be ready…and willing to change.** We must be ready and willing to replace our fears with meaningful changes or behaviors that recategorize fear as we take on the responsibility to protect ourselves from fear. Doing so allows us to effectively redefine ourselves in the ways *we* choose.
- **Do it now!** Right now, begin to take responsibility to find ways to increase your knowledge. Your efforts to gain knowledge provide you with valuable insight leading to awareness. Knowledge connects us with the reasons *why* we have certain fears, making us more aware of ourselves. Awareness lessens fear.

What are some of the ways *you* can begin learning more about yourself? Try these:

- Reading
- Meditating
- Prayer
- Counseling, either professional or talking with a trusted friend or relative.

A great many people suffer from post-traumatic stress that affects the very manner in which they alter their lives to cope with a fearful or traumatic experience. Painful memories continue to haunt them when something in life triggers a memory of the experience. This type of fear can be debilitating and prohibitive to say the least and, more often than not, requires clinical intervention and treatment.

On the flip side, however, many people suffer from the less commonly known *pre*traumatic stress. Having never truly experienced a single negative effect associated with a specific encounter or situation, these people go to great lengths to avoid situations they assume to be harmful or detrimental to their well-being. This presumptive approach to the way we analyze fearful elements can often be just as debilitating as the more common form of anxiety associated with fearful or traumatic experiences.

We must be ready and willing to replace our fears with meaningful changes or behaviors that redefine or recategorize fear as we take on the responsibility to protect ourselves from fear. Doing so allows us to effectively redefine ourselves the way we choose.

Your Belief System Produces Your Reality

If you haven't figured it out by now, the manner in which we perceive a situation matters. In fact, the very course of our life is predicated on the way we react to given situations. If we believe something to be frightening then it will likely present itself in the very manner in which we believe. The fact that it may not be an accurate reflection of the truth is irrelevant.

You have seen it time and again when two people, in very similar situations from very similar backgrounds with no special advantage over each other, produce entirely different results, driven in most part by the decisions they make, the manner in which they react to things, and the attitudes they convey—all fundamental factors that form beliefs. What does this have to do with fear? Everything! While one person decides to accept the results of a painful or traumatic experience as a permanent reality, the other instead chooses to see it as temporary. While one chooses to live in fear, the other refuses to allow the experience to define his life or the construct of his reality. Those who refuse to allow fearful past experiences or a trepidation of the unknown to define their reality (their beliefs) will begin to create a life full of hope and opportunity instead of fear and hesitation.

As promised, these truths would sometimes seem overly simplistic. The simple fact is, most of the intimidation of our fear lies in how we choose to see it. So begin by looking at things more positively, more courageously, more realistically and you, too, will begin to see significant changes manifest right before your very eyes. Some people may even begin to refer to you as *lucky* as they, too, will begin to see significant improvements taking place in your life. You will be consulted, admired, and perhaps envied at how success, happiness, and good fortune just *seem* to be attracted to you.

Most would agree that a positive approach to life is generally the best approach. Yet, some would argue that being positive all the time is unrealistic. The answer to that sentiment is there is no such thing! In fact, reality is relative only unto itself, because when it comes down to it, we create our own reality. If we believe something to be unrealistic then it will indeed be so. We define our own reality through our perceptions, belief systems, and whether or not we *choose* to allow a given situation to define reality for us.

Replacing our fear with knowledge, wisdom, a fresh perspective, and positive thoughts increases our courage, confidence, and convictions and clears a path that *will* allow us to realize our greatest potential. Giving ourselves permission to succeed instills drive and clears an empowering path allowing us to become stronger than fear and doubt while giving us a reason, or a motive, to choose action over apathy.

What kind of experiences have you put aside in your life that fear has taken from you? What dreams and aspirations have you put aside because you are "too old" or because "it's too late"? If this describes you, then perhaps it is time you *replaced* the fear sitting where your experiences and accomplishments belong. After all, what are you *really* afraid of by pursuing these experiences and aspirations? Is it the possibility of finding yourself in an embarrassing situation? Wouldn't that cause too much stress? How should you deal with doubt and difficulties?

The answers to these questions lie within the very questions that are posed. For example, embarrassment and stress are typically compounded as we allow the effects of these factors to take a position of power and dominance over us. Fear takes its hold when we allow it to have free reign of our innermost sanctum—our emotions. What if instead, we expect confidence and courage to emerge? Replacing the two *destructive* elements with two *constructive* elements can have profound and lasting effects on the quality of our lives.

We already know doubt is one of fear's closest accomplices. Think of doubt as fear's pesky little sidekick that should be eliminated with the absolute power you have over it. Doing so will allow you to better deal with fear and everything else it has in its arsenal. Doubt is erased by knowledge, confidence, and wisdom, all of which are empowered by the conviction of our desire to escape our circumstances and enter into a phase of personal renewal the likes of which doubt and fear cannot compete.

By the way, replacing our fears doesn't make them magically disappear. But it will subjugate fear's accomplices and allow you to use the most powerful weapon you have to effectively deal with them—your power of choice.

If you're burdened by a feeling of emptiness, loneliness, frustration, or apathy it should serve as a clear indication that you are off course or out of alignment with your purpose or place in life. I firmly believe the answers to the questions and guidance we seek inherently lie within us. So how do we discover these seemingly elusive answers? We redirect our focus beyond what we can physically see and comprehend to what we can discern spiritually.

Do not allow the word *spiritual* to dissuade you. There are distinct differences between a spiritual connection—having a source of power greater than ourselves—and religion.

The spiritual connection I refer to is one that speaks to our emotional intellect—the all-knowing aspect we all possess. It is a place within ourselves where absolute truth and pure contentment resides. It is also the one place that is connected to infinite wisdom—a place from which answers and inspiration come.

Some refer to this spiritual place as our higher self, God, Chi, the universe, Superconsciousness, inner self, or the center. The various labels we place on this spiritual entity are not as important or as relevant as the fact that, for most of us who have connected with this level of consciousness, we know it to be real and highly relevant. I believe we can all agree there *is* a higher source that fulfills us beyond comprehension, hence its power. It can be accessed through meditation, prayer, or the quiet solitude of contemplation, reflection, and introspection. The plane of consciousness from which it operates provides insight, perspective, and answers that can most effectively put fear in its rightful place of subjugation.

9

The Fourth Truth
Redirect Your Focus

Now that we have established how to look at fear, let's take a look at why we perceive fear the way we do. We will also begin to take steps to redirect or reprogram our subconscious mind to accept a fresh new thought process.

> *"You are very powerful,*
> *provided you know how powerful you are."*
> ~ Yogi Bhajan

Our brains are designed to "help" us avoid danger. The amygdala—the physical part of our brain responsible for processing memory, decision-making, and our emotional responses—are almond-shaped groups of neurons located near the temporal lobes. This brain structure is centrally linked to the emotional responses of both fear and pain. The brain is so fast at processing a reaction to fearful input that we have been known to experience a fearful *reaction* before we are consciously aware of the stimulus. Afraid of snakes? Have you ever experienced an emotional response to anything merely *resembling* a snake? You can thank your amygdala for that.

The issue with a near automatic response to fear arises when we accept the brain's programming of situations we *shouldn't* fear. Imagine having had a fearful childhood experience of say, drowning. The very thought of going anywhere near water would evoke a fearful response most likely limiting our otherwise pleasurable experiences around water of any kind. The amygdala has programmed itself to associate water with fear. The same could be said about a myriad of other preprogrammed experiences we may have faced. The only way to *reprogram* the amygdala is to expose ourselves to the truth or reality of the event that initially programmed the amygdala. We essentially have to convince the brain that our fears are unfounded, that nothing bad will happen, and the fear will be replaced by a new truth.

Change the way you see fear and your life will change. The problem with this statement is that to effect change we must be willing to accept the risk that things will actually change for the better once we summon the courage to replace our fear. The truth is, you do not actually have to *conquer* fear to replace it. You simply have to resist its rather convincing ruse of power and begin to operate on the premise that *you* are in charge. Considering the alternative, the risks are minimal.

As long as we remain committed to our original programming we remain hostage to the very fears created by our programming. What if we were given an opportunity to somehow clear the slate and experience life without preconceived outcomes? Why, virtually anything would be possible, at least until, or *unless,* we discover otherwise. Just think of the possibilities. The truth is, these very possibilities *do* exist. The only issue is that our fears are in our own way. Fear is constantly preventing us from having, being, and doing virtually *anything* we set our minds to.

Step into Mindfulness and Discover a Fresh New Perspective

Mindfulness is not a new concept, but it is a relatively unknown and often overlooked method of seeing things as they truly are. Mindfulness is simply defined as being fully present in the moment. It is the complete and nonjudgmental awareness of the things that are going on around you at any given moment. The awareness of mindfulness reveals life in its truest state—as it is occurring *right now.*

Fear is weakest in the present moment. Most of its power is obtained from what we *perceive* will take place in the future based on the conditioning of our past. If you get nothing else from this book, please remember this—fear is an impostor, a thief whose appearance is often more menacing than reality. Fear's victory lies in convincing you of its overwhelming power, when in fact, its only power lies in the value you assign to it. Those values are deeply rooted in your past experiences and your perception of what may be (the future).

The basis of this philosophy lies in the way our thought processes function. Those of us who tend to see things negatively or second-guess the nature of our own decisions are generally considered to be fear-based thinkers. As negativity dominates our thoughts, negative things are naturally attracted to us. The more this happens, the more cynical and critical we become, seeing things as happening *to* us instead of *through* us. It becomes a perpetual cycle of burden and angst until we resolve to change it. The good news is we *can* change it.

In Order to Effectively Gain Dominance over Our Fears, We Must Make Choices, Not Concessions

All too often we are quick to concede defeat by the very words we speak, the actions we take (or refrain from taking), and the sentiments we convey. Therefore, as mentioned in an earlier chapter, the words we speak, the thoughts we think, and the declarations we make are as important as the approach we take in life. A simple change in our strategy can make a profound difference in the circumstances that are drawn to us as a result.

This new way of thinking, from the core of our existence—our subconscious—will become the basis for new actions we will take to support our desires and objectives. The clarity we gained in the foregoing truths will support the motivation and momentum behind our motives allowing us to operate with confidence knowing we are bigger than our fears, stronger than our fears, and very much in control of the direction our lives take from here on out. When and if circumstances dictate otherwise, we adjust and move on, carrying only the lessons we learn along the way.

The power of redirecting the focus from a self-centered perspective to one of a love-centric (selfless) focus is worth mentioning here. We are most critical of ourselves and therefore tend to position our own self-criticism in such a way that it predominates our ability to operate above fear. The result is typically one preventing us from connecting with others in a meaningful way because of the concerns (fears) we have about our own imperfections. Yet, if we take a moment to get out of our own way by considering the needs of others using the tenets of compassion, sincerity, kindness, and dignity, we adjust the focus away from ourselves and are able to strip fear of yet another tool in its arsenal—self-criticism.

Once our fear is effectively identified, confronted, and replaced with objective-based beliefs and behaviors, it is important we begin to train ourselves to allow *courageous* thoughts to dominate our focus and to be mindful of the things surrounding us at any given moment. In fact, being mindful of the circumstances and conditions of the moment enhances clarity of purpose and serves to put fear in its rightful place of insignificance.

Make no mistake, fear will continually attempt to creep back into our life and will take on many forms to reclaim a place of dominance. It is for that very reason we must continually train our focus on allowing our *purpose* to be a central part of our viewpoint. So how do we do that?

"*Do not dwell in the past; do not dream of the future, concentrate the mind on the present moment.*"
~ Buddha

The mind is an amazing entity. It is physical, yet it is metaphysical. It is generally believed that one aspect of our minds—our subconscious minds —cannot tell the difference between reality and alter-reality. It operates and reacts based on the thoughts we program into it. It doesn't draw distinctions between realistic and unrealistic expectations. The filter of our biases and beliefs govern the limits of our imaginations. Our ability to effectively program our minds to rewire the synapses that perpetuate the programming our biases allow to pass through its filtering process govern our beliefs. This is profound. Understanding this insight will empower you far beyond the prescriptive nature of mastering your fears. You will also experience the beginnings of what is undoubtedly the source of true happiness—knowing yourself.

Do you realize you can literally *choose* to make yourself laugh? Try it. The next time you're alone, stand in front of a mirror. Begin by forcing yourself to laugh. Watch yourself and soon you will literally be laughing at how ridiculous you look and your laughter will transition from a forced exercise to a genuine appreciation for the comedy unfolding in the mirror before you. You're probably smiling right now as you think of this silly exercise. It works. Using this simple "fake it until you make it" approach really works when it comes to convincing your subconscious mind to bring you to places you would rather be instead of places it is currently programmed to take you. As you transition from a force-based exercise to genuine laughter, be quick to recognize the difference in how you feel. The very moment you "feel" connected to happiness is the very moment your subconscious is convinced of your new definition of reality.

Positive thinking requires a commitment and continued practice. In other words, it is not always easy to look at things positively, especially when life isn't exactly fair and equitable. The manner in which life can sometimes throw things at us can be challenging to say the least. But it is precisely during those times when a positive approach can serve us best. Taking such an approach requires courage and a determination to say *no* to fear and see past our circumstances. Look for the good, seek the joy even in the folds of misery. It is there. All you have to do is be still and allow it to reveal itself.

Positive thinking requires maintenance much the same as our bodies require a routine fitness regimen in order to maintain an acceptable level of good health. External sources of positive reinforcement are essential to support our positive intellect. Make it a matter of routine to expose yourself to something positive on a daily basis. If you were out of shape you would seek a trainer or a gym to begin an exercise program. As a minimum you would create an exercise or workout program of your own to at least begin the process. By the way, it's worth noting that, like most worthwhile goals, the process can be a bit painful at first, but the results pay huge dividends to those who are consistently faithful to follow through.

OK, so positive thinking is great, but even I will admit we cannot realistically expect to always *think* our way past our fears. Let's hold on to the notion of positive thinking for a moment while we examine the reasons we tend to act or refrain from acting. I believe once you consider a different perspective, your positive thinking will take you to places you would not have otherwise experienced had you not gained this fresh bit of insight.

The Power of Choice...

Each and every one of us is inherently programmed with an ability to reason. With every choice we face, we weigh the reasons to act or the reasons to resist. In other words, the things that motivate us are driven, in large part, by two emotions: a desire to *gain* something or a desire to *protect* something. With every decision comes an internal evaluation of what the results of our decisions will bring us or how it will protect us. We quickly evaluate whether something we face is worth taking action on or avoiding altogether. The current position of our life has largely been defined by the manner in which we generally approach these kinds of decisions.

Do you allow distractions to easily influence you away from a better or more productive choice? Would you rather sleep in than get up an hour early only to complain there's just not enough time during the day to do the things that bring change (and successful results) into your life? Are you taking on too many things at once, effectively reducing the focus and spreading yourself too thin because of your ad hoc approach to life's priorities and activities?

Humans are motivated by getting, having, and keeping what we need and want. The *getting* and *having* aspect of that statement are force multipliers in terms of bringing us to a point of action, whereas the *keeping* aspect of the statement very often *prevents* us from gaining or experiencing even more because of an underlying fear of potential loss. So how do we "fix" this?

The trick to correcting the conditions keeping us stuck in a state of perpetual stagnation and fear—the cycle that tends to frustrate us the most—is to tap into the convincing strength of our subconscious. All too often our reasons for *not* doing something are simply stronger than our reasons *for* doing it. If we could find a way to reverse the process we would be so much better off, wouldn't we? Well, the simple truth is, it's easier than you might think.

When presented with the question of whether or not we would choose success over failure, I have found the overwhelming response to be success over failure. In fact, I have yet to find anyone who has outright admitted they would prefer to fail. So on a conscious level, we prefer success and everything associated with it (*happiness, anyone?*). Why then are so many people falling short of achieving a level of satisfactory, self-defined success in their lives? Could it be they are allowing fear to convince them they have something to *lose* by standing up and taking the actions that will result in their success? For these folks, the desire for *not* doing something (taking action) is generally stronger than the desire *to* do something to propel their lives forward. Some refer to this as "risk aversion." While there may be some measure of truth to their assessment with respect to a broad analysis, its utility as an identifying trait is subject to dilution when considered in the more narrowly focused context of fear. Rest assured, a fear of loss preventing us from pursuing success is a perception problem that *can* be corrected in order to change the behavioral aspect associated with it, no matter how it is labeled.

To address this fear, one of the first things we should consider doing is to consciously *allow* ourselves to succeed. I have found that giving ourselves permission to succeed penetrates the subconscious with programming that ignites a process of new ideas and reasons for acting on behalf of our desires. We will always have fear and some level of anxiety feeding our desire to procrastinate. "Maybe if I put it off for just a little longer, it won't be as bad," we tell ourselves. But what if I told you the power of choice is so strong, once it is enacted, it initiates a process that awakens the subconscious and ignites forces of change allowing you to escape circumstance and create the life you want? Do I have your attention now?

What would be the *cost* of facing our fears if we were to contrast success and happiness with the choice of allowing fear to rule our lives? What if, instead, we think in terms of what it would "cost" to reach a state of happiness and success in lieu of the alternative? Just thinking about the results of each opposing choice should be enough to help transfer the images (and the drive) from the depths of our subconscious to the forefront of our conscious minds—a place where daily activity takes place, driven by logic, analysis, and stimulus…a place where our dreams are realized.

CAUTION! The precise point at which you begin to experience success is when you may begin to experience…*fear*. This is NORMAL. Your subconscious will sound an alarm that will throw every fear tactic imaginable at you in an effort to get you to stop whatever it is you are doing to create success. Why? Simply because the subconscious mind recognizes it as something new. Don't be discouraged and don't succumb to the fear. The fact that fear has emerged should serve as an *indicator* that you are stepping out of your familiar zone. Fear's objective is to convince you that you have made an error in judgment by courageously taking action to change. Its hope is that you will retreat, second-guessing your own decisions. Meanwhile, your subconscious is waiting for you to make yet another choice. Will you concede to fear and allow it to prevent you from enjoying the fruits of success or will you follow the convictions of your newly discovered personal power? Take a stand and reprogram your subconscious to see fear as an indicator of progress and growth rather than as a reason to second-guess your actions, or worse, stop what you're doing.

There are no predetermined prescriptions for your life. You have the *power* to create the kind of life you envision for yourself. Every one of us has some idea or mental picture—a vision or a story—of how we desire our lives to be structured. If you are currently living your ideal life then you have mastered what it takes to achieve it. If you are not quite where you desire to be then you simply need to clarify your vision, rewrite your story, and reprogram yourself with the tools you need to achieve it. So how do we do that?

A Practical Exercise on Goals…

> ➢ **Choose a destination.** Visualize the utopia defining your ideal life. Use your five senses to help you to define it. What does it look like? What does it feel like? What are the new sensations and experiences that will likely materialize by reaching your destination? These are the fundamental elements of a worthy goal whether it is your desired lifestyle or *any* goal. Write down the details of what you experience as you bring your goals to the forefront of your mind. Put them someplace you will see them every day. Write your own story. And never ever give up on the objective to meet your expectations. Far too many people have given up on their goals because of circumstances. Remember, circumstances do not define us (or our goals). We are more accurately defined by our resolve to overcome circumstance to reach our desired objectives. Circumstance is just another moniker fear uses to disguise itself. Don't allow circumstance to change

or get in the way of your goals. Only *you* should change or adjust your goals, and only because you desire to, not because circumstance dictates.

- **Own your goal.** Claiming ownership of your goal seems simple enough, but far too many people choose erroneous goals based on the expectations or influence of others. Don't get me wrong; there are other people in our lives we must consider—our immediate family, for example—but even they should respect the fact that *you* are part of the overall vision of your collective destination. Once you own your goal, pursue it with passion. The simple truth is you will likely fall short of reaching your goal if you do not create a *burning desire* to achieve it. Life (fear) will throw a great many obstacles or circumstances into your path along the way. Without a burning desire to reach your goals, overcoming those obstacles will seem insurmountable and somehow not worth the fight. Your reasons to *refrain* from taking action will overpower your reasons *for* taking the actions necessary to adapt and overcome.
- **Nurture your goal.** There is nothing more motivating than seeing your goal begin to materialize. An overwhelming confidence begins to emerge as you see some of the elements of your plan take shape. Confidence quiets fear and instills a conviction fear despises. Be mindful that you must continue to nurture your goal with the care and feeding it requires. You must continually watch over it and proactively

guard against all of fear's tactics that are designed to prevent you from realizing your objectives. You *must* keep the burning desire alive and do whatever it takes to reach your goal.

The way I see it, we have two choices that will take us on two totally opposing life courses. Accept fear and live our lives cowered by the oppressive constraints of its ruse, or stand up to fear and enjoy the richness of life with fear residing in its proper place outside the sanctity of our lives. The first thing we must recognize and truly believe is that we *have* a choice. Once we tap into the source of power inherent in all of us we are able to gain a sense of control and dominance over our fears. Amazing things begin to happen at this point. *You* may experience an overwhelming sense of relief, while others may experience a number of other emotions that have escaped them for far too long—freedom, peace, calm, love, forgiveness, joy, insight, etc.

> ***"Mindfulness brings us home to the present and shines a light upon the wonders of now."***
> ~ G. Westfal

Which course will you decide to take? One course keeps us in a continual state of unhappiness as we yield to the deceptive power of fear. The other opens the door to a life full of possibilities unconstrained from the shackles and lies of fear.

10

The Fifth Truth
Be Patient...Be Strong!

Of all human characteristics, patience seems to be the most challenging. Societal influences have conditioned us to expect immediate gratification in just about every aspect we desire, with few exceptions.

It has been said that good things come to those who wait. The wait becomes problematic when we do not take personal responsibility for the actions we must take (or avoid taking) to bring about the good we expect while we wait. While time alone will not change your conditions, you must be ready to embrace change as a process and not an event. Therefore, a level of patience is in order for those actively engaged in bringing about change in their lives.

> *"Patience is bitter but its fruit is sweet."*
> ~ Jean-Jacques Rousseau

Patience is loosely defined as a state of endurance under difficult circumstances calling for perseverance in the face of delay, provocation, or fear, without becoming anxious or annoyed. Another word for patience is *steadfastness*, meaning *consistency* in the face of difficulty or fear. It is consistency that drives defiance of the tactics of fear and defeatism giving way to a just reward to those who persevere. Clarity of purpose, coupled with a burning desire to reach an objective, provides the fundamental infrastructure to patience while consistency is practiced despite circumstance or obstacles.

It has also been said time and again that patience is a virtue. Buddhists regard patience as enlightenment and an ability to control the emotions even when being criticized or attacked or caught in a fearful situation. Those who display patience tend to be regarded as calm and wise and are often seen as having "the gift" of patience. Take heart, however, because patience is not reserved solely for the so-called gifted. Anyone can develop it and use it in most every aspect of their lives, especially when dealing with fear.

In evolutionary psychology, patience is studied as a decision-making process, involving the choice between a small reward in the short term and a more valuable reward in the long term. When confronted with a choice, most people tend to favor short-term rewards over long-term gain. Why? One of the biggest reasons lies behind the immediate gratification factor mentioned earlier. Another reason, just as prolific, is a fundamental fear of loss. We are afraid to delay gratification out of fear we may miss or lose something by waiting.

Two brothers, each having grown up in the same family, having been taught the same values, virtues, and philosophies, venture out into the world. Each one is armed with an ideal objective to bring purpose, value, and wealth to his life among the many other dreams and goals they imbue individually. Both attempt many things according to their individual talents and passions, making mistakes, facing obstacles, and learning lessons along the way. While one brother succeeds in his quest to achieve most of his goals, successfully aligning himself with his purpose while creating wealth in many forms and positively affecting the lives of others along the way, the other succumbs to an acceptance of the circumstances life has dealt him, giving up on his desire to pursue his dreams and ambitions.

The differences in outcome can be attributed to many variables affecting the choices, decisions, and beliefs of each brother. The *principle* difference, however, is that while one brother makes a conscious choice to see past obstacles and to display courage and patience in the face of fear, the other brother accepts circumstance, mediocrity, and impatience as an alternative or reality, allowing fear to select life's course for him. While one brother has the patience to see his way past circumstance, invest his resources, and experience personal growth through patience and understanding, the other succumbs to the frustrations brought on by fear through circumstance and the destructive nature of immediate gratification. I'll leave it to you to decide which brother you believe to be the happier of the two.

Time won't change your conditions, but your strategy will. How many times have you heard someone say something like "Time heals all wounds" or "This too shall pass"? I, too, have said them on occasion. However, these statements, and others like them, are true *only* when accompanied by a cogent strategy. Time alone—that is, time without an *actionable* strategy—will only result in the status quo (or some variation of it). In other words, *nothing* will change until *you* decide on a strategy to bring about change. Just don't forget to act on it once you have a clear plan.

The Patience to Decide…

For many of us, making decisions comes naturally with barely a thought behind the process. For others, the very thought of having to make a decision can elicit fears that can vary from simple anxiety to outright panic or virtually anything in between.

"What if I make the *wrong* decision?" "What if I don't like the choice I make?" These questions are a dead giveaway of our fear of making a mistake. We forget, more often than not, that we actually *learn* by making a choice and, if the situation results in a less-than-desirable outcome, we learn from our mistakes as well. The fear of making a mistake comes from our desire to be as close to perfect as we can be in our decision making. Despite our knowing all too well from the start that rarely, if ever, are we anywhere close to perfection, we still fear having to endure anything short of this seldom-obtained ideal.

Patience can go a long way in the decision-making process. When time and careful consideration are available, we should use the attributes to their fullest extent. Unfortunately, most of us believe that, when faced with a decision, we are somehow compelled to make an expeditious one. If we consider the makeup of the majority of our circumstances we will find that most decisions allow for some degree of latitude when it comes to time and selection. Be patient as you consider your alternatives while being careful *not* to use patience as an excuse (or reason) to avoid a decision altogether.

Trust that your decisions will carry value in the form of insight to the next choice you will face. The real truth is there is seldom a *wrong* choice. All decisions carry *consequences*. Some carry the consequence of victory, accomplishment, joy, and successes while others simply carry the lessons of life compelling us to make adjustments to "get it right" the next time around. Adopt an attitude of "there are no mistakes"—only the *experiences* or *opportunities* that materialize as a result of the courage to make a decision. Indecision is the only other alternative.

Indecision is a warning flag of fear's presence and is a symptom of its hold on the progress and freedoms of your life. You cannot escape the process of choice. Like the concept of "change," choice is inevitable and will happen whether you like it or not because the irony is, even indecision is in and of itself a choice.

A Practical Exercise in Patience through Choice...

Change your perspective—change your life. In order to lessen fear's impact on the decision-making process we are compelled to consider ways to reduce our fear of the unknown. The best way to go about doing this is to change the perspective we have on the process. Instead of seeing choice as a matter of win or lose, we must change our perception to one of win-only. When we find ourselves having to make a choice, we often equate the fate of our decision to its impact on our well-being or financial or social status. We typically fail to see beyond these fundamental elements to the inherent value of the opportunities residing within the results of our decisions, no matter what course we initially take.

"I know that you're afraid...you're afraid of us. You're afraid of change. I don't know the future. I didn't come here to tell you how it's going to end. I came here to tell you how it's going to begin."
~ Neo, *The Matrix*

> ➤ **Adopt a win-only attitude.** The next time you face a difficult decision, do your best to analyze the elements and make the best choice you can, keeping in mind the win-only concept, knowing there are inherent opportunities lying inside virtually every outcome. That's right, regardless of *which* choice you make—right or wrong—there are opportunities for learning, growth,

maturity, love, and happiness. Knowing these opportunities exist provides empowerment, which serves to mitigate fear while instilling hope and courage.

The point behind the win-only concept lies with the valuable lessons to be had literally everywhere, even in the most unlikely or unpredictable places. Even when, or if, we discover undesirable elements inside of opportunity we will find the value of learning what we *don't* want to be of equal value to what we *do* want. Each result or opportunity brings with it lessons that can enhance the quality of our lives. The win-only perspective empowers us to be fearless in the face of an otherwise fearful situation.

Communicate Openly with Others

Seeking the wise counsel of others is one of the best ways to approach difficult decisions. Be careful to discern the difference in "wise" counsel and biased opinion. We all know there are plenty of people who are eager to provide an opinion on something that will have potentially little or no effect on *them* whatsoever. Avoid them if at all possible. Seek only the wise counsel of those who have your best interests in mind. You will know them when you meet them. They are typically well-accomplished, unselfish people who support your desire to embrace the elements that will enhance *your* life, even if it goes against the values held by their own views. They are also the ones who initially respond empathetically with words of encouragement or exude an energy of empowerment.

I serve as a mentor to young men and women in my local community. I can think of no better role to serve than to provide the wise counsel these young people seek. All I ever ask in return from them is to pay it forward as they learn, grow, and mature. In my role as a mentor I strive to instill confidence and empower these young men and women to realize the dreams and desires each of them already has within themselves. It's amazing to watch as they realize they have an *inherent* power to overcome the typical fears we all carry. The communication we share enriches us both as *I* get to witness the effect my wisdom has on them and *they* get to accelerate their journey and avoid a few pitfalls along the way.

Manage Your Expectations

We all create ideal images of what we expect will happen given the circumstances and our selective input in the form of choice or decision. This mental image may or may not have merit once we actually make our initial decision and begin to see results. More often than not, however, our expectations fail to materialize the way we first envisioned them, at least in part. Therefore, it is highly recommended we manage our expectations with caution once a decision is made. Doing this reduces the chance of disappointment and increases the likelihood of success as we watch the results materialize as an *experience* rather than an *expectation*.

Be Strong

The projection of strength can be asserted in a number of ways. The things we perceive internally—those thoughts dominating our minds—are most often expressed by what we say, the physical posture we display, and the manner in which we conduct ourselves—our reactions to circumstances. That said, the *effects* of our strengths are based on the psychological limits we impose upon ourselves and are manifested by how we react to them (physical posture, attitude, etc.).

Strength exudes a sense of power that can sometimes be misconstrued as an arrogant attitude of superiority and control over others. When it comes to conquering our fears, the *power* implied is not one of arrogance but rather one of personal power and dominion over our own fears. This power arms us with an ability to control our actions and perceptions through patience, wisdom, love, and knowledge. It helps us to do whatever is necessary to promote personal growth, to act compassionately, to perpetuate joy, and to love…all from a position of power.

Love and Power Are Inseparable

Love and power go together. To have one without the other is an incongruence that will eventually fail. The assertion of strength when projected toward your fears is an acceptable and recommended approach. Nothing changes without power and will. However, power without love is a reckless approach that can get you into trouble quickly.

For all of its regenerative qualities, absolute power can produce degenerative elements. Power and love typically present themselves as a dilemma rather than a choice. *Don't fall for it.* Selecting a balance by employing both versus one or the other is typically the best approach. In order to yield the best results, both entities (love and power) must equally coexist. The source of bitterness and discord among many relationships arises when there is an imbalance of the elements. Your fears will find no foothold in the wake of a balanced approach to love and power.

I know of a woman who is in an unhealthy relationship. She refuses to step away from the relationship and oftentimes uses justifications to address the fear she has of walking away from it all. The justifications provide a form of "cover" to hide from the real reason she has for remaining in the relationship—fear. The love and attraction that used to define the relationship has been replaced by fear and uncertainty. She has relinquished her power of choice and has subjugated it to her perception of fear. The essence of her fear lies principally in what she perceives she will lose as opposed to what she will gain by leaving. This fear presents itself as one of the strongest deterrents to action and offers a convincing lie about one's personal worth or value. Fear tells her that what she is experiencing in the relationship is "normal." Fear also tells her she will be considered a failure should she decide to walk away. What she has yet to see is how she has refused to take responsibility for her *life experience* and instead has chosen to remain shackled in an unhealthy relationship.

The way we feel toward what we are exposed to in life is a direct reflection of who we are and of how we see ourselves. *Who* we are is reflected in what we value. Our values—especially the values we keep closely guarded—determine our life experiences. The woman I described is the only one who can attest to her personal values. She is not unlike many others I have spoken to who find themselves in this same situation. However, until she takes responsibility for her life experience, the condition or circumstances of her life will go unchanged and she will continue to find unhappiness and discontent. She must love herself first in order to find freedom from her situation. Only when she finds the courage and strength to love herself will she find the resolve (and the power) to change and the ability to offer a balanced love with another, for she will have first discovered herself.

For as many who have *not* found the courage to escape their circumstances—an unhealthy relationship, destructive habits, etc.—there are those who *have* done so. They will be the first to tell you how liberated they feel, despite the presence of fear throughout the transition process. The most significant difference between them and those who have yet to act is an undeniable courage and deeply rooted conviction to change their circumstances. They acknowledged their fear, refused to be subjected to further discontent, and ultimately discovered how happiness is bigger, stronger, and much better than living in fear.

We do not often realize the fear we live with every day until the fear is gone. One of the best ways to handle fear when it presents itself as emotional pain is to openly acknowledge it. This process is a direct assault on fear as it is immediately exposed through identity, confrontation, and an overt intent to replace it with a resolve to face it head-on. When the woman I described finds courage she *will* discover her power. When she discovers her power, she will learn so much more about herself that will reveal empowering traits she may, in fact, experience for the very first time. The personal power will eventually lead to self-love and a knowledge of the many virtues she can offer to a new, perhaps even deeper, more meaningful relationship.

A Practical Exercise on Strength…

- **Create awareness and gratitude.** Awareness supports the notion that we are *present* in the moment and are cognizant of our fear in whatever form it presents itself inasmuch as we are aware of the strengths we have to overcome it. One of the best ways to cultivate gratitude is through a practice of mindfulness. As noted in earlier chapters, being mindful is being fully present in the moment. A mindful presence permits us to take stock of everything we should be grateful for and sets the foundation for increase. Gratitude allows us to pause just long enough to account for the goodness in our lives, *right now*. There is always something to be grateful for, despite our circumstances. Gratitude is an indicator of our readiness and ability to handle an increase whether it be an increase in wealth, responsibility, notoriety, love, or just about any virtue imaginable. Stop and take a look around…right now. What are you grateful for? Study it…experience it… savor it.

- **Tap into your sources.** Our source is that which provides us with what we are looking for in terms of relief, comfort, answers, love, motivation, or a myriad of answers or insight. Some will proclaim their highest source is God or an entity higher than themselves. Suffice it to say, for most of us, our source exists on a spiritual level beyond the realm of our full comprehension, hence the reason we seek its wisdom when we seek answers or comfort or protection. The answers provided by our source become *resources* we use when faced with fearful situations. One of my favorite resources is music. My mind literally rides upon the notes and rhythms of various forms of music as it relaxes and reveals things I would not have otherwise experienced. What is your source, and what are your resources?
- **Meditate.** In truth, there really is no such thing as a "shaky situation." So, anytime you believe you are in such a situation, don't look around or outside of yourself; look *within*. Seek a place of quiet solitude, and spend a few moments in complete relaxation.

Every answer we will ever seek already resides within our grasp. The tricky part is being able to accurately discern those answers. Unlike fear, which presents itself overtly, the answers we seek are on a deeper, more meaningful level and require patience, insight, and awareness. One of the best ways to discover those answers is through meditation.

The meditation process allows us to hear the still, small voice at the center of us all. As stated in an earlier chapter, some call this the voice of God, some refer to it as Chi, while others refer to it as the universe. Whatever you call it, it exists, and it will provide wise counsel for the things you seek.

Meditation places us in direct communication with wisdom and power and puts us at a distance from the daily "noise" that distracts us from our true purpose, intended objectives, desires, and happiness. Fear feeds on the noise whereas courage and convictions thrive on our inner voice of consciousness and reason. Don't neglect the practice of connecting with your center. Avoiding or neglecting it altogether will only lead to perpetual discontent and frustration you can otherwise easily avoid.

- **Be consistent.** One of the best ways to build strength of any kind (physical, emotional, spiritual) is by doing the right thing consistently. Any athlete will tell you they did not build their strength or condition their body overnight or in "six easy steps" as we often hear advertised on television and other media outlets.

No, strength is built upon sound principles of form and consistency.

A firm belief in your objective is an absolute must as there will be times when fear will show up to convince you that your efforts are futile. Frustration may occasionally appear to dissuade you, but if you remain consistent and faithful to your objective, you will become stronger, and you *will* realize the desires of your heart. As you begin to see the possibilities in the impossible, you will begin to see the magnificence as it all comes together.

- **Give.** Giving without expectation will change your life. It will strike a chord within you unlike most any other act you are capable of performing and will provide a return to you beyond your wildest imagination. The universal law of reciprocity supports the notion that whatever you give will be returned to you in greater proportion than you initially provided.

There are more strengths associated with the spirit of giving than any other human trait, save for love, which is so closely associated with giving it is often considered to be one and the same. Giving changes lives, for both the receiver as well as the giver. Givers effect change and deeply affect the lives of others through generosity, compassion, kindness, and counsel. Seek opportunities to give. The return you will experience is not quantifiable but will remain an indelible part of you for the rest of your life.

I receive occasional phone calls, postcards and e-mails from all over the world from the young adults I have had the honor and privilege of mentoring. I mention it not to brag but to emphasize the reach and the powerful effect giving has on both the receiver and the giver, not to mention the world. The contact I receive from those who reach back to acknowledge the role I had in their lives is difficult for me to accurately describe. Suffice it to say, however, I am a changed man because of the experience and the witness of the positive changes I see and hear taking place in their lives. I am empowered by their successes, contributions to their communities, and the effect they have on others as they pay it forward.

Strength, wisdom, and knowledge begets the same. Give and experience something on a profoundly deeper plane of comprehension and experience.

There are still a great many people who fear giving because they fear loss. Giving remains one of the best gifts we can receive. That's right, the simple act of giving actually provides the *giver* an equally gratifying gift. Think of it this way—the outflow you experience by giving not only speaks to the innermost part of who you are but also allows room for *more* to flow back to you. There's that *law of reciprocity* again.

Don't allow the fear of self-preservation or loss keep you from experiencing this truly wonderful transformation. Think of the things you can give that will change lives…yours as well as the lives of others. Then take action. Begin with an objective to change *one* life today. Doing so will most certainly change two—theirs *and* yours.

11

Armed and Prepared

You are now armed with the truth and prepared to confront fear as the thief it is. You are better able to recognize it, are empowered to confront it, and are ready to take a stand against its feeble attempts to rob you of the victories that are rightfully yours. You are stronger, wiser, and able to stand your ground against fear and the deceptive tactics it employs.

Armed with the truth, you have the knowledge and insight to live more courageously and are empowered to realize your true potential. The control you now possess allows you to see fear in its elemental state through renewed insight, increased perspective, and newfound wisdom. Many resources are available that can be applied in the *real* world against *real* fears. Be sure to use this book and the truths it contains as a reference for those times when you need a reminder of just how powerful you are, especially when confronted with a fearful situation.

The value of your renewed perspective is evidenced through the virtue of patience. Do not allow fear's accomplices to convince you that there is safety only within the confines of a book or other valuable resources that must be *quickly* realized. More often than not, *gradual* results will appear as you begin to grasp concepts, principles, and practices. Remember, meaningful change is a *process* and not an event. Keep this in mind as you apply the truths contained in this and other resources as you learn to face your fears courageously.

Clarity Comes by Way of Consistency and Patience

Our imaginations are powerful weapons. If not used carefully, or imaginations can (and most likely will) be used against us. The very things we imagine are *so* convincing to our subconscious minds that we can literally change the tenor of our circumstances by the very thoughts we dwell upon. Fear and anxiety thrive when we imagine the worst. We develop imagination to help us see past circumstances and to perpetuate dreams, goals, and desires. We are free to use our imaginations *any* way we choose. Why then do some people decide to use this power to convey a less-than-desirable message to the subconscious mind?

Maintaining control is essential in the development of a healthy and empowering imagination. Misuse of our imagination is counterproductive to the encouraging factors it is capable of creating. Uncontrollable "runaway" imaginations typically perpetuate doom-and-gloom scenarios fostered by the inevitable "what if" question posed by chronic worriers. It is one thing to be adequately and realistically prepared for the unexpected but quite another to be held captive by oppressive thoughts we allow to become part of the equation. An uncontrollable imagination will inevitably rule our lives through fear and discouragement. These thoughts serve only to rob us of the power to change our circumstances and experience the richness of life. Don't let it happen. You have the *power* to see past your fears if you will just look. What you seek lies just beyond the fray of fear's deception.

Don't allow discouragement to creep in if the results of change do not appear to be taking place at a preconceived or expected rate. Quite often, as we await the evidence of change, the *real* change taking place resides within us and is taking shape whether we are quick to recognize it or not.

I remember the comments I'd get from relatives as I grew up throughout my adolescent years when they would express how much I had changed over time. I never appreciated the changes they saw in me because *I* had hardly noticed any change at all. And so it goes with the changes taking place within us right now. All too often we see change in hindsight, long after it has taken place. The culmination of these changes is typically evidenced by our increasing ability to handle things that used to appear fearful and overwhelming. These changes produce courage, wisdom, knowledge, insight, and other virtues that better prepare us to confront and challenge fear's tactics. The development of these virtues happens over time and better serves our needs in spite of its difficult-to-understand pace.

Remember, any time we step out into anything "new," fear takes notice. It watches us and waits to exploit our vulnerabilities. It is quick to play upon the perceived weaknesses we have until it learns the specific tactics to take to crush our dreams and desires. The next time you detect fear's presence, stop for a moment…look it in the eye and stand tall in defiance of it, knowing you are in control. Your courage will camouflage your vulnerabilities long enough for fear to retreat, leaving you with the benefits of knowledge, wisdom, and personal empowerment as force multipliers you will be able to reuse and summon at will.

The truth is, we all have vulnerabilities. The smart approach to take as we step into the unfamiliar or unknown is to strive to do what is in our power while remaining aware of everything that is not. That may sound overly simplistic and somewhat frustrating, but the fact remains that we cannot control *every* aspect of our lives. Therefore, we should acknowledge the circumstances while remaining conscious of our ability to handle the things associated with those circumstances. The *power* we have to handle circumstance and fear's ensuing lies cannot be overstated. Just being *conscious* of our fear empowers us to interact with it in an entirely new and meaningful way.

There is freedom and power in the five truths outlined in this book. They are not all-encompassing, nor are they intended to be the only considerations you should employ as you address your specific fears. These five truths provide a foundation of knowledge from which to begin to understand fear as the thief it is. They provide a fundamental construct for us to effectively handle life's array of situations and circumstances without compromising our dreams, goals, objectives, and aspirations.

Our knowledge of fear enhances wisdom and overall awareness. As our awareness increases, fear's power effectively and commensurately decreases. Keep this in mind as you contemplate the five fundamental truths…

1. *Identify the Fear*
2. *Confront the Fear*
3. *Replace the Fear*
4. *Redirect Your Focus (Reprogram)*
5. *Be Patient…Be Strong!*

Change takes place every time we expose ourselves to something new and enlightening. It is my belief that, having read the contents of this book, a change has taken place within you. Don't fear it. Embrace it. Expect to see the results of change take effect in your life as you discover new possibilities while knowing fear is in its rightful place at the sidelines of your life.

There is no such thing as futility of effort when it comes to making a personal transformation. Your understanding of fear and the role it plays in your life is a critical element in completing your transformation. Knowledge is power, truth is liberating, and insight is priceless. All three of these elements play an important role in the transformative change that will undoubtedly take place as you expose yourself to a new beginning.

Never forget your ability to overcome, to handle, to persevere, and to achieve happiness. And never forget that…

FEAR Is a Thief!

Speaking with Confidence
An Excerpt, by Larry Waddy

Chapter 2 - Overcoming Fear

Fear Is Not Fatal

Eleanor Roosevelt said the only way to overcome fear is to do the thing we're afraid of. That's true, but like most advice, it's easier to give than to implement. The fear of speaking in public can take on many forms, from a slight dryness of the mouth, to visible tremors, to complete paralysis of mind and body.

At a recent high school awards ceremony, a newly elected school board member was scheduled to give his first public address. He looked a little green around the gills during his introduction and about a minute into his speech he said, "I'm sorry, I'm not feeling very well," and collapsed. Imagine the surprise of the 110-pound woman seated next to him as she tried to catch him before he hit the marble floor.

The good news about performance or communication apprehension (stage fright) is that it's not fatal, although a person may feel that death would be a welcome relief. It can also be controlled.

Training the Butterflies

Our purpose is not to eliminate fear but, as the Toastmasters are fond of saying, to get those butterflies flying in formation. We're striving for grace under pressure, not fearlessness.

What is fear? Psychologists tell us that we are born with only two fears. The fear of sudden, loud noises and the fear of falling are with us from birth. So unless someone in [your] audience is going to set off an explosive, or you're clumsy enough to fall off the podium, you have got nothing to fear. Isn't that right?

Stage Fright

The five basic fears people have are fear of the unknown, fear of change, fear of failure, fear of success, and fear of rejection. When we first speak in public it's normal to feel fear because we're in an abnormal situation. We don't know what's going to happen to us and that can be scary. Once we take that first step, though, the size of the unknown area is much smaller. With each attempt, we reduce the remaining fear until we become comfortable with speaking.

The Physical Signs of Fear

Overcoming [our] fears is not easy, but it *can* be done. The first rule to remember is, as the commercial says, "Never let 'em see you sweat." This may be easier to say than to do, however. Fear causes your heart to race, your face becomes flushed, your hands and knees tremble, your mouth dries, and your brain cells turn to cabbage (well, not literally, but you get the picture, I'm sure). Your body and mind are out of control. To regain control, try the following:

1. **Deep breathing.** Stop taking shallow breaths and start to breathe from deep down in your lungs. Use your diaphragm, place your hand on your stomach and feel the expansion as your lungs fill with life-giving air.
2. **Tense-and-release exercises.** Alternately tighten and release your shoulder muscles, your neck muscles, and your facial muscles until you start to feel the tension ebbing away.
3. **Visualization.** [Begin to] see yourself calm and in control of the situation. See yourself rising and walking confidently to the lectern. Hear yourself speaking calmly and deliberately. See and hear the applause when you finish and walk away with confidence.

In an ancient joke, the tourist asks the streetwise New York cabbie how to get to Carnegie Hall. The wise-cracking cabbie replies, "Practice, man, practice!" Each time you attempt the task, your fear becomes easier. You never get rid of all the tension (fear), but you eventually, through practice, develop enough skill to get the butterflies flying in formation. That's what it's all about.

Our Contributors

Scott Duke is a veteran of the US Air Force and currently serves in Washington, DC, as the Chief of Air Traffic Control, Airspace & Ranges Division at the National Guard Bureau. He is scheduled to retire from civil service in 2016 and plans to move to Arizona, where the fear of not being employed will be his new focus.

Jan Waddy lives in San Antonio, Texas, and is leading a life unrestricted by her former fear of loss. Her joyous nature and charisma keep her busy with friends, causes, and community activities. As a writer, she enjoys poetry and is working on her first publication. She is the widow of Larry Waddy, whose excerpt of his book is included as an addendum to this one and continues to serve as an inspirational source of invaluable wisdom.

About the Author

Gary Westfal burst onto the writing stage when his first critically acclaimed novel, Dream Operative, achieved an Amazon.com No. 1 ranking in the thriller genre in its first year of publication—a phenomenal feat for a first-time novelist. A frequent and lucid dreamer, Gary began documenting his dreams on paper in order to better understand the alter-conscious phenomenon and himself on a deeper level. What began as an exercise in self-prescribed therapy through documentation turned out to be much more than he ever expected and eventually led to the creation and publication of his first novel, followed closely by a second, the critically acclaimed Key Horizon.

Gary publishes his work under his own label, G-Life Enterprises Corp. and creates the concepts for his cover and jacket designs in collaboration with some of the best traditional and graphic artists in the country. His website (www.garywestfal.com) provides visitors with examples of his diversity across several mediums as an artist and his creativity as a writer/novelist. As a speaker, his personality and charisma are contagious attributes, whether in casual one-on-one conversations or speaking to large audiences. His lecture and presentation skills are best described as confident, engaging, and articulate.

He is the creator and chief contributor to *Introspection* (http://gwestfal.blogspot.com/), a periodic blog providing thought-provoking topics seeking to enrich the lives of his readers by challenging them to think more deeply, look within themselves for answers, and be mindful of the value of the present moment. The blog offers a fresh perspective on personal empowerment and covers a wide range of human interest topics while providing a canvas of thoughts and introspection leading to a better understanding of the elements connected to true happiness, balance, and harmony in life. He frequently speaks to audiences about human performance and practical business applications using inspirational narratives. *Fear Is a Thief* is his first nonfiction book.

To be a part of Gary's biweekly inspirational blog and to receive other timely information from him, be sure to visit his website, where you can become part of the conversation with one simple click.

www.ingramcontent.com/pod-product-compliance
Lightning Source LLC
Chambersburg PA
CBHW021127300426
44113CB00006B/319